Supported Housing

This book covers the history of supported housing provision in the context of the broader political and theoretical considerations of the time in which the respective policies were being implemented. The book takes an historical perspective using path dependency as an analytical framework. Particular attention is paid to the critical junctures in the path of supported housing provision and how these limited and continue to limit the policy choices available. The book concludes with a look at the current state of supported housing policy with a view to making recommendations for how policy in this area could be carried forward. The hope is that readers of this book learn the lessons of previous policy initiatives in this area and, by looking at the philosophical underpinning for supported housing, can make recommendations for how it can be funded and provided in the future.

This book provides a valuable resource for scholars and practitioners seeking to both provide and influence policy in this area. It is also a useful source for students studying housing and urban policy.

Yoric Irving-Clarke (PhD) is a researcher for the Chartered Institute of Housing in the UK. He has worked in the provision and management of supported housing for around 20 years.

Routledge Focus on Housing and Philosophy

Routledge Focus offers both established and early-career academics the flexibility to publish cutting-edge commentary on topical issues, policy-focused research, analytical or theoretical innovations, in-depth case studies, or short topics for specialized audiences. The format and speed to market is distinctive. Routledge Focus are 20,000 to 50,000 words and will be published as eBooks, and in Hardback as print on demand.

This book series seeks to develop the links between housing and philosophy. It seeks proposals from academics and policy makers on any aspect of philosophy and its relation to housing. This might include ethics, political and social philosophy, aesthetics, as well as logic, epistemology and metaphysics. All proposals would be expected to apply philosophical rigour to the exploration of housing phenomena, whether this be the policy making process, design, or the manner in which individuals and communities relate to housing. The series seeks an international and comparative focus and is particularly keen to include innovative and distinctly new approaches to the study of housing.

Please contact Peter King (pjking@dmu.ac.uk) with ideas for a book proposal or for further details.

Books in the series:

Thinking on Housing
Words, Memories, Use
Peter King

Social Justice in Contemporary Housing
Applying Rawls' Difference Principle
Helen Taylor

Place and Identity
Home as Performance
Joanna Richardson

Supported Housing
Past, Present and Future
Yoric Irving-Clarke

Supported Housing

Past, Present and Future

Yoric Irving-Clarke

LONDON AND NEW YORK

First published 2019
by Routledge
4 Park Square, Milton Park, Abingdon, Oxon OX14 4RN
605 Third Avenue, New York, NY 10017

First issued in paperback 2023

Routledge is an imprint of the Taylor & Francis Group, an informa business

British Library Cataloguing-in-Publication Data
A catalogue record for this book is available from the British Library

Library of Congress Cataloging-in-Publication Data
Names: Irving-Clarke, Yoric, author.
Title: Supported housing: past, present and future / Yoric Irving-Clarke.
Description: Abingdon, Oxon; New York, NY: Routledge, 2019. |
Series: Routledge focus on housing and philosophy |
Includes bibliographical references.
Identifiers: LCCN 2019002904 | ISBN 9780367110666 (hardback) |
ISBN 9780429024603 (ebook)
Subjects: LCSH: People with disabilities—Housing—Great Britain. |
Public housing—Great Britain. | Housing policy—Great Britain.
Classification: LCC HV1569.2.G7 I78 2019 | DDC 363.50941—dc23
LC record available at https://lccn.loc.gov/2019002904

ISBN: 978-1-03-257063-1 (pbk)
ISBN: 978-0-367-11066-6 (hbk)
ISBN: 978-0-429-02460-3 (ebk)

DOI: 10.1201/9780429024603

Typeset in Baskerville
by codeMantra

Publisher's Note
The publisher has gone to great lengths to ensure the quality of this reprint but
points out that some imperfections in the original copies may be apparent.

Dedicated to C, T and my family

Contents

Acknowledgements

I am grateful to Dr Peter King for his thoughtful and helpful comments throughout and to Dr Beth Watts for her perceptive comments on an early draft of what became Chapter 3.

As ever, I am grateful to Cheri and the rest of my family for their constant support with all that I do.

1 Introduction

Policymakers have long held a conviction that there exists a group of people in society for whom the private housing market will not or cannot provide. This group is usually characterised in terms of poverty or having low incomes. There is a smaller group of people whose needs mean that they are unable to access or sustain housing independently; who need some level of support or assistance to do so. Such people may only need assistance with skills such as budgeting or building the skills to maintain a tenancy and once they have acquired these skills become able to live independently. They may have learning disabilities or long-term mental health issues which means they will never be able to live independently without support. Supported housing has long been one of the several policy responses to this problem.

Present in one guise or another for several centuries, it may not always have been the supportive environment we think of today. Early interventions to prevent poverty focused squarely on punitive measures enforced via the criminal law. More supportive environments were often provided by the charitable donations of the church and wealthy individuals, e.g. almshouses (see Pannell & Thomas, 1999 for a full history).

We are generally familiar with the concepts of poverty and vulnerability. The Oxford Compact Dictionary defines poverty as *"the state of being poor; want of the necessities of life"*; at this point, we could have a discussion about what these "necessities" might be, but for the moment, it would suffice to say that poverty is defined as the lack of ability to provide food, heat, light and clothe oneself as a bare minimum. The same dictionary defines *"vulnerable"* as one *"who may be wounded or harmed; exposed to damage by a weapon, criticism"*; we would all agree that these are commonly accepted definitions and people that fall into these categories are worthy of support from the state.

There are numerous specific definitions of "vulnerability" written into various Acts of Parliament and other policy documents. These mostly relate to defining those that are eligible for various social programmes. Often the problem is not so much one of a lack of definition, but that there are different definitions in different places. Although there is overlap, there seems to be little coordination between these definitions or indeed the services that they are used to mandate. The fact that they have been defined across both the housing and social care policy domains, means that there are often cultural differences in definitions, for example; service user is a fairly innocuous definition in the housing sphere yet in the "mental health" arena it has specific and sometimes stigmatised history. Service users (and professionals) often think of "service users" as "in-patients" in mental health hospitals, and therefore community-based patients object to being identified by the term.

Similarly, one of the problems in talking about "supported housing" is that it is a nebulous term covering a vast range of accommodation types from housing for people with learning disabilities to sheltered housing for older people (which itself has changed its allocation criteria over time). For this reason, Baxter and Carr (2007) recommend treating it as an umbrella term rather than a definition; this is the approach I take in this book. The reason for this is exactly that it is a nebulous-enough term now, and I intend this book to reach back into past centuries to the genesis of services for poor and vulnerable people, into the present and then into the future. Thus, I intend to use it to cover a range of interventions and services.

One general definition of supported housing is the common-sense one – housing that is provided with some element of support (and sometimes care) as an integrated package (Baxter & Carr, 2007). However, Baxter and Carr also feel that this definition lacks the essence of what the sector is trying to achieve. It also fails to encompass the outcomes the sector tries to deliver in favour of process. They add the following elements to the definition:

- A finite resource which is not generally available but limited to those who are vulnerable
- It enables service users to live as independently as possible in their community
- Service users are empowered to become socially included (in the wider sense of community participation)
- The support provided varies and relates to the type of accommodation.

If we compound the two elements, we come to a definition that seems reasonable. Supported housing is therefore housing that meets the criteria of being a finite resource, that empowers service users to become as independent as possible and participate in civic life. The support provided also relates to the specific needs of the people it serves; this is discussed in some detail later in the book.

Social policy has not only been about the regulation of the poor but has also developed to improve and maintain the fitness of the population. It has not only protected the working classes from the worst excesses of capitalism but also allowed them to benefit from it (Dean, 2008). In the UK, the movement from liberalism to social democracy, to Conservatism via (to some degree) socialism (Drake, 2001) has coloured the nature of what support is provided, how it is provided and who provides it. These have often been characterised as right- vs. left-wing debates, but the situation is more nuanced than that. As suggested above, such discussions involve the concept of fairness, what is considered just and how this reflects the wider relationship between state and individual, the social contract. The idea that the individual gives up some of their freedoms in return for the protection and mediation of disputes by the state. Given that people who require some level of support often require greater protections and have great difficulty enforcing their rights, these issues become even more pertinent for them.

What follows focuses on the theoretical-practical issues facing policy-makers at the time of writing. The book provides a multifaceted framework for policy analysis; first, via using a path dependency framework to examine how the policy history of supported housing and how limits policy options in the present; second, using McConnell's (2010) heuristic for looking at "policy success" to provide an independent framework for analysing how successful the policies have been in relation to the three domains McConnell outlines; and finally, using an ideological and philosophical framework. Analysing public policy is a notoriously difficult task, and we are often left reliant on the goals set forward by politicians and policymakers when we come to look at how successful a given policy has been. These goals are often unclear, ambiguous or change considerably during implementation; the Supporting People policy (2003–2010) is a good example with a string of documents adding new goals and morphing the existing ones (see Irving-Clarke, 2016). McConnell's heuristic provides an independent set of criteria by which we can begin to look at the success or failure of a given policy. Programme success is clearly important (meeting policy goals), and McConnell adds "process" and "political" to this, process meaning the smooth progress of a piece of legislation through the parliamentary process and the political meaning "does it enhance the popularity or electoral prospects of the government?"

Whilst important, these domains in themselves are insufficient, I would suggest, to fully assess the impact and success of a policy. Whilst McConnell's heuristic addresses the "3 Ps" – programme, process and politics – I suggest here that there is a fourth "P", the philosophical. Whilst McConnell's domains provide vital and interesting lenses to look at policy thoroughly, they omit an important area, that of fairness, justice and to what an acceptable relationship between individual and state should be. Is it not possible for a policy to meet its stated aims, pass smoothly through the legislative process, be a popular policy but still be highly authoritarian? The widespread use of CCTV may be one such policy. It might well reduce crime or enhance prosecution or conviction rates; its widespread use suggests process is not an issue and it is popular with the public as it gives a, perhaps illusory, sense of safety to the public. Yet, libertarians rightly raise concerns about its use, how justifiable is it to surveil the everyday actions of wholly innocent people on the basis of a possibility that the state might record a crime and successfully prosecute the person responsible?

Also, the resources of the state are limited, and decisions must be made about what and who limited resources should be spent on. Thus, political debate is often not about whether help should be given, but rather about who deserves the allocation of scarce resources. Where Nozick (1974) argues that justice can only be based on the freedom and fairness of transactions in the free market, Rawls (1971), whilst also concerned with this, pays greater attention to effects and outcomes being fair or just; Sen (1992) and Nussbaum (2000) discuss those resources needed for good human functioning and how they might be provided. There are serious considerations regarding justice, fairness and freedom that must be debated.

Chapter 2 provides a toolkit for the analysis of supported living policy for the rest of the book. Chapter 3 provides the ideological frameworks that have been in place during the time supported housing has been in existence and a philosophical framework for analysing success or failure of policy not only on its own terms, but also in terms of the relationship between state and individual, ethics and justice. Chapter 4 provides a thorough history of the provision of care and support in the UK using the path dependency framework set out in Chapter 2. It also looks at the main reasons why supported living has failed to build the adequate policies and institutions to secure the funding and longevity that other policy areas, e.g. health or education have. Chapter 5 closes the book by making recommendations on the future of policy in this area based on what goes before. The chapters intersect in terms of the history of supported housing, ideologies and implementation of policy, and it is very much intended that they should be read in conjunction with one another.

References

Baxter, S & Carr, H (2007) *Supported Housing and the Law*, SITRA, London.
Dean, H (2008) *Social Policy*, Polity Press, Cambridge.
Drake, RF (2001) *The Principles of Social Policy*, Palgrave, Basingstoke.

Irving-Clarke (2016) *Supporting people – How did we get here and what does it mean for the future?* Unpublished PhD thesis, De Montfort University, Leicester.

McConnell, A (2010) *Policy Success: Rethinking Public Policy*, MacMillan, London.

Nozick, R (1974) *Anarchy, State and Utopia*, Basic Books, New York.

Nussbaum, M (2000) *Women and Human Development: The Capabilities Approach*, Cambridge University Press, Cambridge.

Pannell & Thomas (1999) *Almshouses into the Next Millennium: Paternalism, Partnership, Progress*, Policy Press, Bristol.

Rawls, J (1971) *A Theory of Justice*, Harvard University Press, Cambridge, MA, USA.

Sen, A (1992) *Inequality Re-examined*, Oxford University Press, Oxford.

2   Looking at policy – a toolkit

Introduction

Policies are implemented for a number of reasons. These may be to keep things as they are, to effect change, to privilege a specific group or treat all equally, to promote equality or extend inequality, to promote a set of values or accommodate diverse values or to change individuals/groups or to change environments (Drake, 2001).

This chapter examines the three areas of theory (in relation to supported housing) that I will be using in the rest of the book. First, path dependence, the suggestion that the policy options available at any given time are limited in type and range by decisions taken in the past, the time, place and context in which they are implemented – and that these in turn limit the options available to future policymakers. Policies to provide support and/ or accommodation for the poor and vulnerable have been in existence for centuries and so lend themselves well to this type of analysis.

Second, that the way in which policies have been implemented has changed over time and line with political demands and ideology, and that this has also had a profound effect on what is desirable and possible; third, that we require a way of assessing to what degree a given policy has succeeded or failed – here I outline one such framework. Finally, I look at the role that ideology and philosophy play in policymaking and how these considerations help us assess and shape policy.

History matters

Pierson (2004) (cited in Pollitt [2008]) argues that political science and the social sciences in particular have become increasingly decontextualised; that analysis has moved away from historical explanations of phenomena. Researchers and implementers (e.g. civil servants, voluntary sector providers) have instead chosen to make policy on the basis of recent experience and the reasons why the existing system doesn't work without reference to the historical precedents that led to its introduction. Pollitt (2008) is critical of this focus on the present and future viewing it as "… *deeply destructive of our understanding*" and stating that it "…*impoverishes our academic theories and infantilises our policy and management responses*" (p. 29). He identifies that there are at least two ways in which time could be an important consideration for policymakers.

First, where events in the past impose significant constraints or costs on the present choices such as generational change (e.g. the imminent disappearance of "baby-boomers" from public services) or cultural change (e.g. shifting public confidence and trust in government – organisational culture can also be seen as a constraint from the past [Wilson, 1989 cited in Pollitt, 2008]).

Second, where planning for some present or future action means that some elements of a programme are bound to take a long time, e.g. fundamental organisational restructuring, training professional staff (doctors, lawyers, teachers, social workers, but it could just as easily apply to staff working in housing), building new political coalitions to support new programmes or carrying out complex international negotiations. Some policies simply take a long time to implement and their impact on the public sector is probably very large (Pollitt, 2008). There are also some contexts in which cycling, or alternations are typical. Hood (1998, p. 191) notes the "*apparent tendency for public management systems in time to produce their polar opposites*".

Pollitt (2008) makes the point that in situations where multiple of these factors are involved, the process is "…*horrendously complex*" (p. 19) and should therefore be approached with some caution. This caution is essential to complex policy areas such as care and support for the vulnerable – it is hard to think of a policy area where it is more important to get it right. This being so, the following section looks at path dependency and how this can provide a basis from which to analyse the past policy decisions taken in care and support policy. Given that past policymakers have far from got it right, the past provides us with a good place to start looking for lessons for the future.

Explaining path dependency

There are situations in which events in the past are crucial to the feasibility of current options. Pollitt (2008) gives the extreme example of "irreversibility", but this could also apply to circumstances where the costs of reversal are so high as to make it an unviable if not impossible option; there are less rigid versions of path dependency though. This section looks at "strong" path dependency and direct link of cause and effect, followed by soft path dependency – a more useful theory in terms of policy and finally concepts used in path dependency such as "policies", "institutions" and "culture" that can act to bind future decision-making.

Bengtsson and Ruonavaara (2010, p. 194) give Sewell's definition as a starting point: "*...what has happened at an earlier point in time will affect the possible outcomes of a sequence of events occurring at a later point in time*". Strong path dependence clearly links cause and effect. Malpass (2011) defines the "strong" version of path dependency as a situation where it is implicit that the more steps one takes along a given path; the harder it is to return or change direction. Pierson (2000) uses the concept of "increasing returns" to illustrate this point. This could be the increasing return on an investment of time, money or effort, or could represent the increasing costs of changing course. This is a useful concept in that it makes the point that once a particular path has been embarked upon it can be difficult to go back. The increasing returns argument struggles to explain how periods of change are precipitated, however.

In an attempt to do so, Streeck and Thelen (2005) argue that change can often result from an accumulation of gradual and incremental change. They go on to suggest several ways in which change can occur without the need for shock, whether internal or exogenous. First, the slowly rising salience of subordinate institutions to usurp the dominant (displacement), new elements may attach to the existing institutions gradually changing their status and structure (layering), neglect of institutional maintenance in spite of external change results in slippage in institutional practice on the ground (drift), a redeployment of old institutions to new purposes whilst still attached to old structures (conversion) or a gradual withering away of institutions over time (exhaustion).

Strong path dependence explanations may be good for looking at entrenched institutions such as government, churches and charities, but policy is much less entrenched than these organisations (Malpass, 2011); it should therefore be treated with caution when dealing with the analysis of policy (Bengtsson & Ruonavaara, 2010; Malpass, 2011). Marsh and Rhodes (1992) point out that the concept of "increasing returns" (from Pierson) must also be treated with caution. They make the observation that rather than getting stronger over time, most policies fail; they therefore conclude that it is the diminishing returns of a policy that make change more likely and not less.

Bengtsson and Ruonavaara (2010), in relation to the study of public policy, offer a "weak" concept of path dependency where "*...one event, which is more or less contingent, considerably changes the probability of subsequent events or outcomes*" (p. 195). This is an important theoretical development as it widens the scope of path dependency from one of simply cause and effect (the strong version) to a definition where events can be contingent but still determine future events, and makes this a matter of degrees rather than an either/or equation. They also go on to make three points about path dependency that underpins their own analysis (of Nordic housing). First, there is a possibility that

> …single events, which are not the product of larger social forces or trends, might be influential to societal outcomes. This could even involve some element of chance. Secondly, previous events might be distant in time to the outcomes that are explained by them. Thirdly, as the process is "essentially historical", it can only be analysed historically, that is by paying special attention to the temporally ordered sequence of events that leads to the outcome.
>
> Bengtsson and Ruonavaara (2010, p. 195)

Their understanding of path dependence sees that policy decisions at point A set the rules of the political game at point B between the actors involved, and this in turn creates a self-perpetuating chain of "…*games between actors, institutional change, new games, new institutions etc.*" (p. 195). They also state that the key variables of path dependency can be summarised as efficiency, legitimacy and power. This means "…*events at point A would make some alternatives appear either to be more efficient, more legitimate, or more powerful at point B*" (p. 195).

This moves us beyond simple cause and effect, accepting that chance or contingent events can be part of a path-dependent process. The only way to truly determine the full picture is to conduct a holistic, historical analysis in order to see the emerging patterns. However, it is also not enough to assume that all policy (or any other) development is path dependent. Kay (2005) is clear about this stating:

> The observation that change has been limited over a period of time is not sufficient to infer a path dependent process: an unconstrained but stable series of choices would be consistent with this observation. In order to demonstrate constrained change, and thus identify a path dependent process, it is also necessary to show that what did not happen could not have happened – that is certain options were not feasible because of earlier sequences of decisions.
>
> (p. 554)

To help us, Kay (2005) suggests that there are two key variables that can be seen as path dependent: policies and institutions. He states that this is an important distinction and argues that whilst policies are about operationalising change, institutions are about governing behaviour by constraint, that is to say that individuals and groups "…*act in a context that is collectively constrained, and these restraints take the form of institutions"* (p. 555). He also makes the point that in using path dependency as an analytical tool, we must define what we mean by both policies and institutions.

Policies

There is no easy definition of policy. Kay (2005) refers to one definition *"anything that a government chooses to do or not to do"* (Dye, 1972, p. 2). Although broad, it does at least make the point that government can choose to do, or not to do, anything it wishes and that doing nothing can equally be seen as a legitimate choice. The point of studying path dependency therefore is to theorise which factors have restricted the choice or behaviour of the government, how and for what reasons. As Kay (2005) states, *"…there is no unique policy level or scale but rather several levels that may be examined as policy"* (p. 556). As one would expect, numerous definitions of policy have been given. Heclo (1972) states that *"…policy is usually considered to apply to something 'bigger' than particular decisions, but 'smaller' than general social movements. Thus, policy, in terms of levels of analysis, is a concept placed roughly in the mid-range"* (p. 84).

Kay (2005) identifies the *"policy system"* as the first scale in this mid-range (p. 556). He states that whilst this is a broad definition, it is possible to see policy in this sense and observe change at the macro level. However, he also sees that policy at this level is a complex variable comprising many elements, subsystems and actors and that the real empirical challenge for an observer of policy change is to identify what specifically about a policy is path dependent; policy subsystems can equally be understood by using path dependency. Rose and Davies (1994) and Hall (1993) are useful in this regard. The former regard the "policy programme" as being the basic unit of analysis; defining this as,

> …a specific combination of laws, commitments, appropriations, organisations and personnel directed towards a more or less clearly defined set of goals. In other terms, this is a policy instrument; an identifiable tool or resource of government used for a specific set of purposes. This is a more finely grained perspective than the policy subsystem.
>
> (p. 557)

Hall (1993) sets out three orders of policy change: change in the level of policy instruments (first order), change in the instruments actually used (second order) and change in the overall policy paradigm (third order). Hall's (1993) typology suggests that policy change and policy stability can be observed simultaneously in the same policy paradigm but at different levels.

…logical distinctions between changes in things and changes in kind to be made in terms of policy. It gives us categories of things (policy instruments and their different levels) and kind (policy paradigm). This allows us to see whether an existing policy is changing or whether a new policy is being introduced.

(Kay [2005], p. 557)

Kay goes on to point out that

It is incumbent upon scholars using the concept, whether theoretically or empirically, to be clear about in which sense the term policy is being used: in particular, which scale of perspective is being adopted – the level of the whole or particular constituent elements of a policy or to policy level institutions?

(p. 558)

By seeing policy as being able to change on different levels (or orders), we can observe and explain change on all these levels using different theories. We can also see that change at one level does not mean contemporaneous change in others. For example, we might ask how much the easily observable systems change within Supporting People really changed practice on the front line.

Institutions

Kay (2005) offers Hall and Taylor's (1996) definition of institutions as a starting point:

…the formal or informal procedures, routines, norms and conventions embedded in the organisational structure of the polity or political economy. They can range from the rules of constitutional order to the conventions covering trade union behaviour or bank-firm relations.

(p. 938)

Kay (2005) identifies three levels of institution that are *"regularly distinguished"* (p. 555). First, the macro or constitutional level; second, the collective choice or policy decision level; and lastly, the operational level of individual decisions. Kay also accepts that past policy decisions can also be classed as institutions in that they can *"…act as structures that can limit or shape policy options"* (p. 557). This seems to suggest that he settles on this as a definition of institutions in the understanding of policy development as path dependent. Put simply, anything that constrains or limits future policy options.

There is debate about whether policies in themselves can be institutions that is to say they can limit options or prevent change in and of themselves. Malpass (2011) suggests that policies can be seen as institutions, saying they are *"...social arrangements that structure and shape actions and behaviour"* (p. 4). However, he goes on to distinguish between several different layers of institutions that are embedded more or less deeply in society. He suggests that the most deeply embedded institutions are those such as the family, marriage, religion and the market, followed by the welfare state and social housing as less entrenched. He is also clear that these need to be conceptually separate from *"institutions as organisations"* (p. 5) such as government departments, companies, churches and charities.

Limits of path dependency

It is important to note that path dependency is not in itself a theory that can be used to explain phenomena (Bengtsson, 2008; Kay, 2005). Rather, it is a mechanism for observing *"...a historical pattern where a certain outcome can be traced back to a particular set of events on the basis of empirical observation guided by some social theory"* (Bengtsson, 2008, p. 5).

Malpass (2011) is critical of both versions of path dependency in that they both imply that there is a reducing chance of change the further one progresses down a given path. We know that policies change over time and so, as Malpass suggests, a more nuanced version of path dependence is required to counter this. Pierson (2000) also acknowledges that the concept of *"increasing returns"* offers an *"overly static view of the social world"* (p. 265) and suggests that *"...path dependent analysis need not imply that a particular alternative is locked in following the move to a self-reinforcing path"* (p. 265).

However, Kay (2005) is generally supportive of path dependency as an analytic technique. He argues that it is an appealing concept for policy scholars as it captures the idea that once implemented policies can be difficult to change or reform. He also points out that it provides an insight that policy decisions accumulate over time and that there can be a *"...process of accretion that restricts the options for future policy makers"* (p. 558). He is also positive about path dependency in that it encourages a dynamic analysis, that is to say that time is an independent variable in the explanation of change rather than a dependent one where change occurs via some *"...change in initial parameters or an exogenous shock"* (p. 559). Finally, Kay sees that path dependency has the advantage of being flexible in the explanation of change. Kay (2005) uses a quote from North (1990, pp. 98–99) that states,

> At every step of the way there are choices – political and economic – that provide...real alternatives. Path dependence is way to narrow

conceptually the choice set and [to] link decision-making through time. It is not a story of inevitability where past neatly predicts future.

Path dependence then is a process that emphasises stability and continuity between key events. The first key event may not be easily identifiable, and it is an "axiom" of path dependency that small, contingent events can have large consequences over time; indeed, it is the timing of these events that separate them from other similarly small events that have little or no impact (Malpass, 2011). Baumgartner and Jones (1993) introduce the idea of a *"punctuated equilibrium"* where periods of prolonged stability are separated by short and intense episodes of change.

Having established time, place and context as key to the development of policy, I now move on to look at some of the ways in which to practically approach the analysis. Pollitt (2008) makes the point that there is no one set of specific methods for conducting such research but considers basic chronologies essential to any serious analysis of policy history. A chronology should cover the appearance, sequence and duration of key events – only then, Pollitt contends, can analysis of paths, punctuations and cycles begin. Bengtsson and Ruonavaara's (2010) suggestion is that we look at events backwards (starting at point B). They argue that in doing this, it is possible to view events at point B (those possibilities that were implemented, discarded or not even considered), in the light of events at point A (the original policy decision) and then theorise *"…what type of mechanism has been at work between the two events."* (p. 196). This chronology is provided in Chapter 4.

The following sections of this chapter continue the analytic framework for the rest of the book. First, the various ways that policy can be implemented by administrators followed by a framework for independently evaluating policy success.

How is policy implemented?

Beyond the ways in which time and policy decisions limit or open up policy options in the present, the way in which policy is implemented and evaluated also has an impact. This is one of the lenses I will be using to explain what has been happening in the policy area under discussion. At the outset of supported housing policy (and many other policy areas), implementation was often carried out directly by the state via either the criminal law or local government. This section tracks the history of implementation and how policy has been implemented, concluding with a discussion of a recent framework for evaluating policy success – this will be used later in the book with reference to supported housing policy.

Top-down implementation

Early attempts to provide accommodation, care and support for the vulnerable were frequently carried out by state actors (see Chapter 4 for a detailed history). Implementation was carried out via "Weberian" bureaucracy with policy goals and prescribed actions flowing "top down" from policymakers to implementers. Top-down theories are useful in that they place government at the forefront of the process and in democracies such as the UK, this can only be correct. Why should policymakers not be able to control the actions of those charged with implementing policy? It is the government who will be held accountable should the policy fail, not those charged with implementing the policy.

Top-down theory sees policy implementation starting with policy formulation at government level with those implementing policy (administrators) following through on policy intentions and delivering services that meet these intentions. Van Meter and Horn (1975) define the implementation process as "*Those actions by public or private individuals (or groups) that are directed at the achievement of objectives set forth in prior policy decisions*" (p. 445). Top-down thinkers emphasise the importance of separating formulation and implementation processes and then concentrate on what can go wrong between policy formulation and delivery of outputs and how policymakers can control this.

Looking at implementation within the American federal system, Pressman and Wildavsky (1973) spend much time analysing the extent to which implementation depends upon relationships at local level. They argue that a number of even small relationship breakdowns at this level can mean large deficits in the success of implementation; hence they introduce the idea of an "implementation deficit"; stating that the degree of cooperation between implementing agencies must be close to 100% in order for implementation to be considered successful. Minimising "implementation deficit" is the task in hand. Hood (1976) theorises that we can do this by

> …thinking about what perfect administration would be like…perfect administration could be defined as a condition in which 'external' elements of resource availability and political acceptability combine with 'administration' to produce perfect policy implementation.
>
> (p. 6)

The top-down approach is not without problems, however. It champions the interests of policymakers over the interests of those implementing the policy and those the policy directly affects. Although from an accountability point of view this may be desirable, it cannot really be believed that a small group of policymakers in government can understand the subtle complexities and issues of front-line practice and the interaction of the public with implementers. The top-down approach is also open to criticism for its lack of flexibility in dealing with complex social issues. If and when it becomes apparent that a given policy is not working in the intended fashion, how can the process be amended without recourse to policymakers again? How long might this take and what guarantee is there that their subsequent attempts will fare any better?

The bottom-up approach

Top-down approaches had dominated thus far due to the prevalence of monolithic government departments being responsible for delivering policy objectives (in the UK at least), thus allowing a large (but not total) degree of control of implementation by political masters. However, in federal systems, such as the US and increasingly the UK, policy is implemented by a variety of agencies external to government (the development of policy networks is discussed later).

Bottom-up theorists see policy as being enacted at street level via interactions with the target group. Lipsky (1980) puts forward a theory of "street level bureaucracy". This states that front-line workers formulate policy through their interactions with the public. Lipsky does not place the power of implementation totally in the hands of those at street level. He sees those implementing policy on the ground or what he terms "street level bureaucrats" as an alienated group (p. 76) and decisions made at street level as often being a result of the coping mechanisms they are forced to employ as an overworked and underfunded workforce. For example, with reference to knife crime, if the Home Office issues a "zero-tolerance" policy on knife-carrying mandating all those found with knives to be charged, but an overworked police force continues to issue "police-cautions" to knife-carriers, what then is the policy? Is it that which politicians decree, or the actual actions of the police?

For this reason, Lipsky's work makes the point that it is futile to study top-down implementation when greater efforts to control from the top only serve to frustrate those at the bottom and cause greater problems. Therefore, other ways are needed to secure the accountability and cooperation of those at street level, including the public that policy will affect.

This introduces the idea that those delivering policy are more than just drones doing as they are told by policymakers but play an active role in creating and implementing policy and may also deliberately frustrate policymakers or subvert policy. Theorists such as Hjern and Porter (1981) Hjern and Hull (1982) and Barrett and Fudge (1981a, 1981b, 1981c) went on to develop Lipsky's (1980) basic idea of policy being created at street level arguing that studies of implementation must take account of the formal and informal relationships between implementing agencies and the actions of those at street level. In such a situation, compromise by policymakers can be a tool to obtain policy objectives, top-down theory would view such an action as a loss of control and therefore a failure (Barrett & Fudge, 1981a, 1981b, 1981c). To use the example given above, in not charging all people caught carrying knives with an offence, the police may be responding to a lack of resources that allows them to do so, prioritising the most serious offenders. A bottom-up view would take account of this complexity and may mean the provision of additional resources or allowance of discretion over which charges to pursue in the hands of the police. The inability of the police to charge all offenders would not be seen as failure.

The "bottom-up" approach sees that implementation is necessarily complex and requires a much more nuanced and pragmatic approach to implementation than prescribed by the "top-down" school. The next section looks at the synthesis of these two approaches to implementation.

The synthesisers

A third school of thought has sprung from the two discussed above, inevitably, this next stage in the development of theories of implementation was an attempt to synthesise the top-down and bottom-up approaches taking the best of both and accepting that it was necessary to use both in order to make sense of a complex implementation processes.

Elmore (1980) suggests that the study of complicated events requires the use of more than one theoretical approach. He is critical of theorists who are all too willing to criticise but reticent to offer solutions. He offers "backward mapping" as such a solution. As the name suggests, backward mapping starts at the lowest possible level of the implementation structure (where administrative actions intersect with personal choices) with a statement of the specific behaviour that generates the need for a policy. Only once this is done does the analysis state a policy objective, this is given as a set of organisational operations and then as outcomes that will stem from these operations. The analysis then backs up through the implementation structure asking two questions at each level. What is the ability of this unit to affect the behaviour that is the target of the policy? And, what resources does this unit require to have that effect?

The policymaker must then devise a policy that directs resources at the units likely to have the greatest effect. What Elmore (1980) observes is the necessity to see implementation as something that happens at the front line without forgetting that policymakers have an interest in ensuring that they can influence outputs. Elmore acknowledges that there are both top-down and bottom-up pressures on implementation, that "policy" is the best method of achieving objectives rather than the potential use of softer options to create a changed policy environment. However, his suggested model focuses on the allocation of resources rather than the achievement of objectives.

To use our example again, if the policy goal is to reduce the number of people carrying knives, the policymaker would ask himself "who can have the greatest effect" and "what resources do they need to act?" The answer, after analysis, may well be that front-line officers can have the greatest effect by charging and prosecuting all offenders; suitable resources would therefore be allocated to them.

As suggested above, the ways in which public policy is implemented in Britain have changed. Weberian ideas about bureaucracy and account-ability (government) have faded and theories about how government can set up and manipulate networks (governance) have become the new ortho-doxy. Rhodes (1997) notes that this move to a *"differentiated polity"* (p. 4) has been in train since 1945. Hill and Hupe (2002) note that these ideas are particularly important to the British experience as UK government has a history of fostering policy networks in order to implement its policy goals. The following section, then, looks at the development of policy networks.

Policy networks

The change from the use of government actors to the use of policy net-works should be seen as a move from 'government' to 'governance', or as Osbourne and Goebbler (1992) put it, *"the transformation of the public sector involves less government (rowing) but more governance (steering)"* (p. 34). Hill and Hupe (2002) offer several different definitions and types of governance from the basic to the complex but all agreeing that the basic definition is a "super-system" intended to deliver outcomes via constituent subsystems.

> Governance…is concerned with creating the conditions for ordered rules and collective action, often including agents in the private and non-profit sectors, as well as within the public sector. The essence of governance is its focus on governing mechanisms – grants, contracts, agreements – that do not rest solely on the authority and sanctions of government.
>
> Milward and Provan (1995) quoted in
> Hill and Hupe (2002, p. 3)

Ripley and Franklyn (1982) inject some political realism into the equation regarding the policy deficits (from top-down theory) as inevitable and im-plementation processes, necessarily complicated. They also recognise the implementation process as necessarily politicised and that different players in the game have their own agendas.

> Implementation processes involve many important actors holding diffuse and competing goals who work within a context of an increasingly large and complex mix of government programs that require participation from numerous layers and units of government and who are affected by powerful factors beyond their control.
>
> Ripley and Franklyn (1982, p. 9)

There is no longer a clear line of accountability between policymakers and service deliverers. Instead there is a complex panoply of policymakers, statutory, voluntary and private sector service deliverers, think-tanks, politicians, service user groups and service users, regulators, funders and other interested parties that play a role in the delivery of services, in this case supported housing/living services. Interactions between these implementing agencies are neither hierarchically structured nor logical.

The consequences of these changes are several. Hill and Hupe (2002) note a necessity to now distinguish between government and governance, structures and processes, institutions and activities, and locus and focus. This means that for the researcher looking at implementation, there is no longer a linear policy to delivery connection; rather, the multiplicity of actors means that relationships operate up, down and across networks, and therefore there is a need to define fairly precisely who they are looking at, what they are supposed to be doing and how this impacts upon the end service user in conceptualising any study or part thereof. Or as Hill and Hupe (2002) note, governance is now broadened into a "…*multidisciplinary, multi-level and multi-focus exercise looking at a multiplicity of actors, loci and layers*" (p. 16).

If we use our example of knife-carriers again, rather than solely relying on the police and criminal law to deal with the problem, implementers might look at the range of charities, voluntary sector organisations and others that work with young people in order to prevent them from carrying knives in the first place. Using the network of such organisations, the government can prevent knife-carrying to a large extent, thus leaving the police to deal with only the worst offenders. Supported housing services are often viewed as just such a preventative service.

This section has set forward theories regarding policy implementation as a lens through which to view the historical and path-dependent history of supported housing. As pointed out, path dependency is not an evaluative framework, so I now move on to examine a framework (McConnell, 2010) for evaluating the success of policies in this area (and others).

Assessing policy success

One of the problems for students of policy is finding ways to measure success without relying on only the original or modified policy aims as a yardstick or relying upon claims by politicians about the success of a given policy (Marsh & McConnell, 2010; McConnell 2010). There are widespread claims about the success of given policies by interested political parties whether they be observers, journalists, politicians, bloggers or academics (Marsh & McConnell, 2010). Little work has been done to create "...*any systematic criteria for assessing success or failure*" (*ibid*, p. 565). Focusing upon recent trends for delivering public-sector improvement, they acknowledge an apparent abundance of evaluation studies but contend that these can only take us so far when looking at policy success.

Building on the work of Boyne (2003) and Bovens et al. (2001), Marsh and McConnell (2010) and McConnell (2010) propose their own heuristic, providing a useful starting point for beginning to assess the relative success of policy initiatives. Retaining programme success (did the policy deliver as intended?) and political success (did it help the government in political terms?) (from Boyne and Bovens, respectively), McConnell (2010) adds process success. This is concerned with the way the problems are defined, options examined, stakeholders consulted and decisions made. McConnell notes that there are some areas where policymaking does not conform to the "*sequenced and rational assumptions of the policy cycle*" (p. 41) and therefore can be driven by self-interest of political actors, locked in by path dependencies or the policy agenda managed in advance. His contention is that this makes it even more important to include process, as it is important in both practical and symbolic terms. I begin then with process.

Process success

He identifies several dimensions of process that may be examined. First, that the policy goals are preserved throughout the process. This acknowledges that there is a policy process (often legislative) that can and does make changes to the policy by scrutinising and amending it. The passage of a policy through this process with no or minimal changes can be perceived as a success from the policymaker's point of view.

Second, does the policy ensure political legitimacy for the government? This aspect can broadly be summed up as "does the government have the right to do this?" McConnell (2010) suggests that policies that have been through a "*constitutional or quasi-constitutional*" (p. 41) process will have a large amount of legitimacy conferred upon them. Even where policies are contested, McConnell argues, this very debate can confer legitimacy as such debate is at the heart of the democratic process.

Third, the building of strong and legitimate support for a policy can be seen as a success. Gaining the support of Parliament and on the floor of the house is a key consideration for any legislation. McConnell (2010) suggests that policies without the support of a strong coalition are more likely to be derailed by minor failures.

Finally, does the policy symbolise innovation and influence? McConnell (2010) suggests that merely tackling old problems in new ways can confer success upon a policy initiative. In this, he includes policies brought in from other jurisdictions to solve policy problems (policy transfer).

Programme success

In this dimension, success is based on outcomes and evidence rather than political ideology. Again, several domains are identified.

First, did the policy do what it set out to? This focuses on the bureaucratic delivery of outcomes. McConnell (2010) highlights that in both American and European terms, the focus is upon delivering the agreed objectives set down when the policy was approved. Therefore, this can also include implementing policy in accordance with intentions as well as the sole delivery of outcomes.

Second (and relatedly), did the policy produce the desired results? Did the policy have a positive impact on society? McConnell (2010) states that outcomes and objectives sometimes overlap, but this is not necessarily so.

Third, did the policy benefit the target group? Some policies are targeted at a specific group(s) and success can be measured by the benefit that a given policy brings to that group. This could be a group based upon issues such as class, territory, gender, religion or race. McConnell (2010) also points out (importantly) that policies may at the same time, have a beneficial or deleterious effect on a given group. Indeed, some policies are designed to do so.

Lastly, did the policy meet the policy domain criteria? There are numerous policy domains that McConnell (2010) identifies. Health, energy, industry, agriculture and defence are some that he names specifically. All these domains have a degree of shared values that are held by the majority of actors in those policy communities. McConnell (2010) suggests that these values are often enshrined in industry standards or benchmarks. These may include risk management standards, accounting standards, best value standards; McConnell also includes efficiency standards in this group.

Political success

Governments do not just oversee the implementation of policy, but they also do politics. McConnell (2010) suggests that there are two broad definitions of "politics". The first dealing with generic issues of conflict and cooperation, the second (and more relevant) is that focusing on policymaking arenas, parties, lobby groups, elected representatives and bureaucrats. He is clear that it is this second definition that he is referring to. Further, he narrows the definition down to dealing with "…*government, its capacity to govern, the values it seeks to promote and so on…*" (p. 50). Political success is divided into the following areas.

First, does the policy enhance electoral prospects? It is reasonable to assume that an elected government wishes to stay elected. Any policy that enhances this prospect can reasonably be considered successful in this context.

Second, can the government control the policy agenda and ease the business of government? McConnell (2010) contends that governments face a difficult task. They are faced with omnibus problems, some chronic and long-standing, others short term; they are lobbied by many groups and individuals who have conflicting views and are constantly scrutinised by an often hostile media, political opponents and others. Therefore, he also contends that governments must control the policy agenda and may conceivably produce policies that may not solve the policy problems presented but sustain their capacity to govern. Therefore he argues that a programme may be considered politically successful if it involves a narrow definition of the problem in order to make it manageable (Rochefort & Cobb [1994] quoted by McConnell [2010, p. 51]), gives the appearance of dealing with a problem – this might involve a "token" or "placebo" policy or help buy off/counter critics or gain support from key interests/actors through concessions or promises of future reform.

Finally, does the policy help sustain the broad values and direction of government? McConnell (2010) contends that a party without vision will never be elected to government. It can therefore be said that policies may be considered successful if they align and/or promote this vision or the direction of government. McConnell (2010) also identifies a variation on this theme where a government may want to explicitly signal a change in direction, forging new values and a new direction. Such policies help open policy windows and legitimate further reforms.

Limits of the heuristic

McConnell's (2010) and Marsh and McConnell's (2010) model is helpful in that it moves the debate on from one of failure (that tended to define success as merely the absence of failure) to one of attempting to define and assess what is successful about policies and to what degree. It also moves on to acknowledge that policy success is not only about delivering outcomes but also about success in terms of process and politics. However, the heuristic is not without its limitations; these are examined below.

First, in terms of "programme" success, we are left reliant upon the policy-makers' stated aims and objectives for a given policy. It is therefore incumbent upon us to ask ourselves if these are the honest goals of the policy or is there some hidden or wider agenda? And, even if the policy meets its objectives, does that mean success? When Tony Blair announced a policy of no person having to wait more than 48 hours for an appointment with a GP, GPs merely stopped making appointments more than 48 hours into the future. Although the policy goal was largely met, can it be considered a success? In this same vein, policies often have unintended consequences, for better and for worse. Only studying the policy objectives would risk ignoring these unintended effects even where these were of benefit to the success of the policy.

Second in terms of "process" success, this is defined as keeping the policy in close to its original form throughout the legislative process and moving through this process smoothly. This defines a policy as something that is enacted by a piece of legislation and this is not so for all policies; how then, should these policies be assessed?

The parliamentary process in the UK is predicated upon improving or changing legislation as passes through the House of Commons and Lords before receiving Royal Assent. The issue here is that any policy or piece of legislation is likely to be amended and this is not necessarily a bad thing; a policy may be more successful as a result of amendments. It may therefore be more useful to examine the amendments made and how they affect the implementation and programmatic success; the current model tends to treat amendments as a bad thing, even where they are helpful overall. Also, just because a piece of legislation moves quickly through the process and received minimal amendments, is this necessarily positive? A good example of this is the *Dangerous Dogs Act 1991* passed extremely quickly on the back of several serious dog attacks. This piece of legislation was passed through Parliament very quickly but is now accepted by most as an unworkable law that does not deal with the problems of dangerous dog breeds. In terms of process, this would be seen as a success; however, a longer time spent on scrutiny and amendment may well have made this a better piece of law.

The third of McConnell's (2010) criteria is political success – has the policy supported the overall direction of the government and made them more popular/electable than before? Again, this is a highly contested, subjective area. Testing success in this way might be problematic where governments are passing legislation that is unpopular, but they think that it is going to contribute to the greater good. One example of this would be the reforms that the Thatcher governments of 1979 onwards passed that transformed many areas of life in the UK. Many of these reforms were unpopular with

Thatcher heading for defeat at her first general election as an incumbent but are now viewed by many as necessary and successful reforms.

It may not be useful to think that just because something is unpopular it is a failure of policy; the reverse may also be true. These judgements are also subject to temporal factors (Pollitt, 2008), a policy judged a failure in early evaluations might be judged a success later on once the policy has had time to bed in and become effective. It is therefore important to consider success as a longitudinal factor rather than as a static one-off judgement.

Conclusion

This chapter has established that time and temporal factors are an important dimension of policymaking and development (Pollitt, 2008). This book uses path dependency as a framework to analyse the development of policy over time, there is support for this approach by several theorists such as Kay (2005) and Pierson (2000). In doing this there are several questions that should be asked; which events in the past, recent or distant, small or large, contingent or planned have shaped the development of a given policy? What has been the effect of these events and over what timescale? What levels of policy are being examined, and have there been similar, different or no change at different levels? I will also be looking the history of supported housing through the lens of implementation styles discussed and in terms of political ideology and philosophy.

This book particularly concerns itself with Kay's (2005) concepts of "policies" and "institutions", defining these in the case of care and support, and looking at how these have acted to influence and constrain policymaking in this area. To do this, Chapter 4 constructs a detailed history of policy time for care and support and draws out some of the issues that have supported or bedeviled policymakers. It also looks at the main events that have influenced care and support policy, some planned, some contingent; and the effects these have had over policy and action in this area. And, most crucially what the effects are of path dependencies and constraints of policies and institutions on the policy under examination.

References

Barrett, SM & Fudge, C (1981a) Examining the policy action relationship in SM Barrett & C Fudge (eds) *Policy and Action: Essays on the Implementation of Public Policy*, Methuen, London pp. 3–34.

Barrett, SM & Fudge, C (1981b) Reconstructing the field of analysis in SM Barrett & C Fudge (eds) *Policy and Action: Essays on the Implementation of Public Policy*, Methuen, London pp. 249–278.

Barrett, SM & Fudge, C (eds) (1981c) *Policy and Action: Essays on the Implementation of Public Policy*, Methuen, London.

Baumgartner, FR & Jones, BP (1993) *Agendas and Instability in American Politics*, University of Chicago Press, Chicago.

Bengtsson, B (2008) *Why so different? Housing regimes and path dependence in five Nordic countries.* Paper presented at the ENHR International Research conference "Shrinking cities, Sprawling Suburbs, Changing Countrysides" Dublin 6–9 July 2008.

Bengtsson, B & Ruonavaara, H (2010) Introduction to the Special Issue: Path dependence in housing in housing, *Theory and Society* 27(3) pp. 193–203.

Bovens, M et al. (2001) Does public accountability work? As assessment tool, *Public Administration* 86(1) pp. 225–242.

Boyne, GA (2003) What is public service improvement?, *Public Administration* 81(2) pp. 211–227.

Drake, RF (2001) *The Principles of Social Policy*, Palgrave, Basingstoke.

Elmore, RF (1980) Backward mapping: Implementation research and policy decisions, *Political Science Quarterly* 94(4) pp. 601–616.

Hall, PA (1993) Policy paradigms, social learning and the state: The case of economic policy making in Britain, *Comparative Politics* 25(3) pp. 275–296.

Hall, P & Taylor, D (1996) Political science and three new institutionalisations, *Political Studies* 44(5) pp. 936–957.

Heclo, HH (1972) Policy analysis, *British Journal of Political Science*, 2(1) pp. 83–108.

Hill, M & Hupe, P (2002) *Implementing Public Policy*, Sage Publications, London.

Hjern, B & Hull, C (1982) Implementation research as European constitutionalism, *European Journal of Political Research* 10(2) pp. 105–115.

Hjern, B & Porter, D (1981) Implementation structures: A new unit of administrative analysis, *Organization Studies* 2(3) pp. 211–227.

Hood, CC (1976) *The Limits of Administration*, John Wiley, London.

Hood, CC (1998) A public management for all seasons, *Public Administration* 69(1) pp. 3–19.

Kay, A (2005) A critique of the use of path dependency in policy studies, *Public Administration* 83(3) pp. 553–571.

Lipsky, M (1980) *Street Level Bureaucracy: Dilemmas of the Individual in Public Services*, Russell Sage Foundation, New York.

Malpass, P (2011) Path dependence and the measurement of change in housing policy, *Housing Theory and Society* 28(4) pp. 305–319.

Marsh, D & McConnell, A (2010) Towards a framework for establishing policy success, *Public Administration* 88(2) pp. 564–583.

Marsh, D & Rhodes, RAW (1992) *Policy Networks in British Government*, Clarendon Press, Wooton-Under-Edge.

McConnell, A (2010) *Policy Success: Rethinking Public Policy*, MacMillan, London.

Milward, H & Provan, H (1995) A preliminary theory of interorganisational network effectiveness: A comparative study of four community mental health systems, *Administrative Science Quarterly* 40(1) pp. 1–33.

Osbourne, DE & Gaebler, TA (1992) *Reinventing Government: How the Entrepreneurial Spirit is Transforming the Public Sector*, Addison-Wesley, Reading, MA.

Pierson, P (2000) Increasing returns, path dependence and the study of politics, *American Political Science Review* 94(2) pp. 251–267.

Pierson, P (2004) *Politics in Time: History, Institutions and Social Analysis*, Princeton University Press, New Jersey.

Pollitt, C (2008) *Time, Policy, Management: Governing with the Past*, Oxford University Press, Oxford.

Pressman, JL & Wildavsky, A. (1973) *Implementation*, University of California Press, Berkeley.

Rhodes, RAW (1997) *Understanding Governance: Policy Networks, Governance, Reflexivity and Accountability*, OU Press, Buckingham.

Ripley, RB & Franklyn, GA (1982) *Bureaucracy and Policy Implementation*, Dorsey Press, Homewood, ILL.

Rochefort, D & Cobb, R (1994) *The Politics of Problem Definition: Shaping the Policy Agenda*, University Press of Kansas, Kansas.

Rose, R & Davies, PL (1994) *Inheritance in Public Policy: Change without Choice in Britain*, Yale University Press, New Haven, CT.

Streeck, W & Thelen, KA (2005) *Beyond Continuity: Institutional Change in Political Economies*, Oxford University Press, Oxford.

Van Meter, D & Van Horn, CE (1975) The policy implementation process: A conceptual framework, *Administration and Society* 6(4) pp. 445–488.

Wilson, J (1989) *What Government Agencies Do and Why They Do It*, Basic Books, New York.

3   Philosophy, ideology and supported housing

Introduction

This chapter acknowledges and discusses a second highly formative influence on policy, the prevailing philosophy and ideology at the time that the policy is formed and implemented. I suggest here that one of the key themes in the history of supported housing (as outlined earlier) is the relationship between individual and state, and that the path of those requiring support has been one of a gradual overturning of a "Leviathan"-like (Hobbes, 1651) state apparatus that has gradually acquiesced to demands for individuality. My contention here is that the manner in which supported housing is provided is a good proxy for the overall conceptualisation of the relationship between individual and state. As this has developed from the highly paternalistic (from the divine right of kings and post-war consensus) to a more individualistic social arrangement (via Thatcherism and the Third Way), so has the nature of provision for those considered vulnerable.

One of the problems of discussing policy in relation to supported housing is that for much of the time there hasn't been a coherent one. The earliest attempts to deal with paupers was to criminalise them and set up a paternalistic system that was designed to disincentivise poverty by making the situation of paupers as dire as possible. This was reflected in early punishments (the stocks) for those that could not afford to support themselves and in subsequent solutions such as the workhouse and asylums. Both places you would not want to end up in, perhaps brutal, perhaps neglectful; very likely both. Services for the poor and vulnerable grew piecemeal with various pieces of legislation adding (in top-down fashion) to the permissions and duties of local authorities to meet people's needs. The fact that these were mostly in the form of permissions that could be ignored by cash-strapped local authorities was not helpful. Where duties were conferred these were often poorly implemented. Policy is often split into several periods where there has been a coherent approach. The principle guiding philosophies behind the social contract and then the First, Second and Third Ways are discussed here.

Philosophy and housing

As King (2011) points out, theory and practice are often uncomfortable bedfellows within the study of "housing", and I suggest the welfare sector also. Theory is often seen as an *"indulgence that should not be undertaken whilst serious issues such as homelessness persist"* (*ibid*, p. 109) or is often ignored by theorists as a practical matter not suitable for theorising. Political theory is rarely applied to housing or welfare issues and where it is, is often consequential in nature. It is applied to a given policy in relation to the outcomes that it produces.

For example, Taylor (2018) applies a modified version of Rawls' (1971) difference principle to Housing First and the "Bedroom Tax" respectively concluding that the new duties it imposes do not meet the terms of her revised test. Likewise, Watts and Fitzpatrick (2018) argue that policy regarding welfare conditionality should be judged from multiple philosophical viewpoints, e.g. utilitarianism, contractualism, social justice. Their focus though remains on outcomes for those subject to conditionality – what the policies' effects are at street level.

This is not meant as a criticism, these are more than legitimate subjects for political philosophers. Plato, Kant, Hobbes, Hegel, Rousseau and others have all been concerned with outcomes for the people living in the "state"; whether this be a city state or a larger modern country. The consequences of an action or policy are not enough to tell us whether it is justified or acceptable. Jeremy Bentham's "utilitarianism" states that the most important factor in any decision is that it maximise aggregate happiness or pleasure. Not the happiness of the individual or any one group, but the aggregate sum of happiness of those affected. There is some disagreement about how this should be defined.

Different theorists have focused upon concepts as diverse as happiness, desire, well-being, pleasure (Goodin, 1993), whilst others focus on the minimisation of suffering (Smart & Williams, 1973). Utilitarianism requires equal weight to be given to each person's interests (Kymlicka, 2002) and the acceptance of the concept of *declining marginal utility*; that a person will derive less utility from the second unit of a good than the first (Watts & Fitzpatrick, 2018). The gains and/or losses of those who have the least are also weighted more heavily (Goodin, 1993); meeting the needs of those who have the least first is an important and often ignored aspect of utilitarian thought.

Thus, in the well-known example, if a train is running out of control and will hit another stationary train and the only way to prevent this is for a person to lie on the track, diverting the train over the points onto a parallel track but being killed in the process, that person should sacrifice themselves. The happiness of the many people on the stationary train outweighs the grief caused by the single death. Utilitarians would find it justifiable for the state to coerce the person to lie on the tracks – increasing aggregate happiness being the only right thing to do. Clearly, we would recoil from this suggestion. The state (rightly) does not have the power to compel the death of a citizen in these circumstances, regardless of how happy it might make others.

The consequences of a given policy are clearly not enough to justify certain actions. It is therefore important to consider the relationship between the individual and the state when formulating policy and making decisions and what we consider the appropriate relationship to be. Plato, for example, finds that society should be structured rigidly with all acting according to their talents, children removed (by the state) from their parents at a young age and trained according to their skillset (Plato, 2007). Although we would never countenance such a method today (has anyone?) Plato's formulation is intended to promote meritocracy, but clearly makes for tyranny. Living a "good life" or being happy is not enough. If others are to have power over us, there need to be constraints over how and when they can use that power and to what degree.

Before the "enlightenment" and the Glorious Revolution of 1688 that introduced parliamentary sovereignty, the UK was an absolute monarchy. The system of governance was feudal in nature, most of the land owned by the monarch or feudal "lords of the manor" with the majority of people subject to the rule of these literal "landlords". The thesis of the divine right of kings (see Filmer, 1680) held that the monarch was placed on the throne by God and therefore held the "divine right" to rule over his dominion as he/she saw fit.

The people at this time were viewed as the "subjects" of monarchy, often the figurative children of the sovereign, entrusted by God to their care. This led to a highly paternalistic system of support with what support was available being in the gift of the monarch or their representative – who could be tyrannical or benign as they wished. By paternalism we mean the coercion or "nudging" welfare recipients into compliance with behavioural norms to protect them from the consequences of their own poor decision-making (Watts & Fitzpatrick, 2018). This is done out of beneficent concern for their welfare (Scoccia, 2008).

This frequently took the form of measures that were hardly supportive, being put in the stocks for three days and removed forcibly from the parish being the standard policy response. These measures of "hard paternalism" have been reflected more recently in the work of Lawrence Mead (an American conservative). Mead (1992) contends that welfare recipients are not self-regarding, rational actors but require stern action from a tutelary state to move from welfare to work (or at least off welfare) in order to meet society's normative expectations (Watts & Fitzpatrick, 2018). Mead's hard paternalism shows clear reflection of the "liberal" period's attitude to the destitute. Mead's views are also represented in later periods.

Throughout the period characterised by the "poor laws" support for paupers remained on a paternalistic basis. Whether Houses of Industry or Correction, workhouses or asylums, the focus of housing for the poor remained brutal with a clear focus on preventing poverty by providing an incentive to stay out of this inadequate and punitive provision. There were signs of utilitarianism also. The creation of asylums to house those who were disruptive or incapable of working points to a policy that prizes the well-being of the majority over the minority of those who do not or cannot conform. This is also reflected in the not unconnected Victorian eugenicist movement. The expanding field of genetics held intelligence as an innate characteristic and raised concern over the high birth rate amongst the poorest groups in society (Means et al., 2008). The idea that this could lead to a contamination of the genetic stock of the country led to "defectives" being removed from society and placed in asylums to prevent them from reproducing (*ibid*). The rights of the minority, once again, taking second place to the well-being of the majority.

There are reflections of this state paternalism in current welfare policy. The welfare reforms introduced by the coalition and continued by the Conservatives are at least partly based upon the idea that people must be coerced into behaving in the way that the government deems correct. The conditionality associated with welfare reform allows the government to completely withdraw benefits for periods of up to two years threatening those sanctioned with destitution and very possibly homelessness. Whilst it would be a stretch to say that they would be cast completely into a state of nature (as per Hobbes) as they would still have the protection of the police and National Health Service (NHS), for example, it is hard to escape the thought that destitution (a key feature of the state of nature) is being employed as a coercive tool to ensure that welfare recipients behave "correctly".

During the enlightenment the idea of a "social contract" became popular, often thought of as the quintessence of this relationship. The following section looks at the development of these ideas and their application to supported housing.

The social contract

This can broadly be thought of as a grand, unwritten bargain between the individual and the state whereby the individual gives up certain freedoms in return for protection and support from the state apparatus. Such a bargain is the basis for the state's authority over the citizenry and for the enforcement of civil rights under the law of the land (in Locke's [1690] conception). Before Locke, Thomas Hobbes set out his conception of the social contract, which is laid out in his masterwork "Leviathan" (Hobbes, 1651).

Hobbes contends that without the protection of the state there exists a "state of nature". Life in this state of nature is without mercy; indeed, Hobbes sees it as *"solitary, poor, nasty, brutish and short"* (Warburton, 2014), no less than a state of war. There is no arbiter of fairness or justice nor any means of redress for those who feel themselves wronged. If this is the state of nature, Hobbes contends, people have strong reason to avoid it. Having lived through the carnage of the English Civil War, Hobbes is of the view that even the most tyrannical sovereign is preferable. Hobbes' sympathies are for a monarchy (rule by a single individual) although he is not sympathetic to Filmer's (1680) divine right of kings thesis (Warburton, 2014). He also allows for rule by a representative group of the wider society (democracy) or a subgroup of a smaller pre-eminent group in society (aristocracy), in any case he considers that the power of the sovereign or sovereign group must be absolute to deliver upon the (tacit) promises made in the social contract.

Although Hobbes' vision of the state of nature has been criticised for being unduly pessimistic about human nature, it is based upon some plausible normative assumptions. If all people have the right to all things, this is an invitation to conflict. Some resources will be desirable and/or scarce and so there will be competition to obtain them. People might make pre-emptive strikes to protect their assets thus inviting violence, or an individual or group of power-hungry persons may seek to dominate others and make them subservient. This is without considering disagreements about religion, moral values and which sports team is the best. Fortunately, Hobbes thinks that we also possess the means to escape this condition. A shared view that peace is good and therefore the means to achieve peace are also good. These rules impel us to submit to a sovereign force and seek peace with others under the auspices of such (as described above).

John Locke (1690) took a different view of rights and therefore the social contract. After challenging Sir Robert Filmer's "divine right of kings" thesis in his first treatise on government, dismissing the idea of a god-imposed sovereign, in his second treatise Locke asks "why should we obey our rulers? And, under what circumstances might we be justified in opposing them?" (Warburton, 2014).

Like Hobbes, Locke sets forth his own conceptual "state of nature". Unlike Hobbes' dystopian view, Locke imagines that people are bound by the "laws of nature" and these prohibit causing harm to others and themselves. This stems from his belief that God intends us to live out our natural lifespan, all are equal before God and therefore no person has the right to dominate or harm another. He therefore contends that in the state of nature, aggression against another is open to be punished either by that person, or any other person or persons who observe the transgression.

Like Hobbes, Locke believed that individuals could give up some of the rights they have in the state of nature, e.g. the right to punish others for breaking the laws of nature and transfer these to a sovereign authority in return for protection and the greater safety of the political community. Power to make laws and punish others is transferred to the hands of an individual or a small group entrusted to act for the common good. Further, Locke sees that where an individual or government abuses their power and becomes tyrannical, they give up the consent of the ruled and are asking to be overthrown; rebellion becomes not only acceptable but essential. All government is therefore government by tacit consent.

Jean-Jacque Rousseau (1762) agrees with Hobbes and Locke on the practice of a social contract; that it is in the interests of people to form a political entity or a "state" for protection and to resolve disputes civilly. Where Rousseau departs from Hobbes and Locke is where he attempts to explain how a people may form such an entity but not give up their freedom to act as they wish, which he also prizes greatly. To do this, he puts forward his concept of the general will. Rousseau's concept of the general will should be thought of as that course of action which is in the best interests of society. It should not be confused with the "will of all" (Warburton, 2014). Warburton gives the following example.

Where the will of all the members of society is that taxes should be lowered (to enable them to keep more of their own money), this is the "will of all" – to reduce taxes. However, if it is in the interests of society that taxes remain high, that is the "general will" even though it is not the wish of individual members of society. Those that do not wish to comply with the general will (pay high taxes) must be "forced to be free". Freedom for Rousseau lies in complying with the general will, not pursuing one's own personal caprice. It should also be noted here that there is a significant difference of opinion between Locke and Rousseau. Where Locke believes the state exists to guard the life, liberty and property of the individual, Rousseau's "general will" thesis prizes the overall good of the political community. Thus, where there is a conflict between the rights of the individual and the group, Locke believes the rights of the individual are prime, whereas Rousseau says that the rights of the group take precedence.

There are of course several convincing criticisms of social contract theory. First, that the existence of a social contract presupposes a social order (de Maistre, 1996), why would people come together if they didn't already know and trust one another and know that they had a common interest? Godwin (1793) outlines four other objections to the social contract. These are that first, it is iniquitous to bind future generations by the contract agreed to by earlier ones. If it is required that I submit to the social arrangements in place at my birth, what is the basis for that agreement? Surely it can't be the mere agreement of my father(s) to the arrangement?

Second, Godwin contends that the tacit consent of the governed is not enough to confer authority on the government. If mere acquiescence of the governed is all that is required, then even the most tyrannical of governments is legitimated by this acquiescence. Acquiescence does not, therefore equal consent for Godwin. Third, Godwin objects on the grounds of the length of the contract. His point here is that consent to be governed by a given set of laws may be given at an express point in time. Indeed, it might even have once been possible to present all the laws in folio to individuals and gain their express consent. However, Godwin's objections are that first, this is no longer practical or possible and second, that consent given once (or tacitly) is taken to be consent for all time. Not only consent to abide by the laws on the books at the time, but also all future laws without any hint of what prohibitions they might contain. This criticism is particularly pertinent in the UK where there is no written constitution to bind parliament. In the American tradition, it could at least be argued that consent to be governed is based on the individual and the state upholding the terms of the constitution and the bill of rights; with the courts acting as arbiters of what is constitutional and therefore binding on the populous. Finally, Godwin objects to the social contract on the grounds that if government derives its authority from the consent of the governed, then (assuming tacit consent is not enough) the government can have no authority over any person that does not give their consent.

However, despite these objections it is clear that something approaching a social contract exists. There is broad agreement that some state intervention is necessary to provide social order and protect people's "rights", it is the degree of this intervention that is at issue. Where Hobbes believes that even a tyrannical sovereign is preferable to the state of nature, Locke believes that the power of the sovereign should be limited to those actions that promote the common good. The question here is therefore how can we ascertain what that common good is? This is where more consequentialist philosophers are useful. As discussed above, Jeremy Bentham set forward that the correct consequence of action should be to maximise the aggregate of happiness or well-being in society, but as we also established, this can have perverse consequences in some situations.

How then are we to approach ascertaining the extent of this intervention? This is something that modern philosophers have considered at length. Perhaps the most illustrative here is to compare Rawls' *A Theory of Justice* (1971) and Nozick's *Anarchy, State and Utopia* (1974).

A theory of justice

In *A Theory of Justice*, Rawls invites us to consider what a just society might look like. He does this via a thought experiment where we are placed behind a "veil of ignorance" that removes our knowledge of our own gender, employment status, intelligence and aptitudes etc.; whilst leaving us with knowledge of politics, economics, the basis of human organisation and human psychology. From this *"original position"*, we set out the general principles upon which we would want society to be organised. From this position Rawls sets out two such principles, one based on liberty, the other on distribution of goods/wealth.

Rawls states that from behind the "veil of ignorance", we would want everyone to have the same basic liberties compatible with ensuring liberty for all. This means that you would have the right to speak freely, have freedom of conscience, religion and association – the rights we are generally familiar with. However, these rights end where they curtail the rights of others. The intervention of the state via the rule of law is justified in these circumstances to prevent the rights of others being violated. As Rawls orders these rights lexically, this right must first be satisfied before moving to the next.

Equality of opportunity and the difference principle

Second, Rawls states that inequality related to certain offices or jobs can only exist where these jobs are open to all, that none are excluded on spurious grounds, e.g. age, gender and sexual preference. Rawls also goes further than this, including the provision of education and training to allow people to meet their potential as requirements. The second part of Rawls' conception is the difference principle. This states that inequality is only acceptable in circumstances where the worst off are in as good a position as they can be.

For example, in her book *Social Justice in Contemporary Housing*, Taylor (2018) modifies Rawls' basic tests as stated above to replace the "wealth" factor of inequality and replaces it with the possession of agency to make and pursue the individual's conception of a good life. In doing this she contrasts two contemporary housing policies, the Bedroom Tax and Housing First. The first of these policies states that if a household living in a property with more bedrooms than the government deems they need, they must have their housing benefit reduced. This acts as an incentive for them downsize to a more suitable property, thus freeing the larger property for a family that needs it. People over the eligible age for pension credit were exempted.

The impact of the bedroom tax has been manifestly harmful and has not addressed its own policy goals; aside from the human cost, downsizing has not occurred as expected and the policy has failed across a range of indicators (see Gibb, 2015; Moffatt et al., 2015 for assessments). Taylor (2018) contends that the deleterious effects of the bedroom tax on people's lives means that they are not able to formulate or pursue their own conception of a good life, the policy therefore fails her philosophical test for whether it is ethical – the policy should therefore be discarded.

She contrasts this with Housing First. This is a policy that provides housing and support to people on an unconditional basis. Under this model both housing and wrap-around support are provided to the individual on the basis that first they will be accommodated regardless of their behaviour and whether or not they pay rent or the associated accommodation charge. Likewise, support is provided on the basis that people are able to access on their own terms and when they feel ready to do so. Taylor provides evidence from evaluative studies that people who have used Housing First state that it has given them their lives back. It has allowed them to regain agency over their own lives, come to their own conception of a "good life" and pursue this in a way that suits them. Housing First therefore passes Taylor's modified Rawlsian test and is therefore considered to be a policy that should be pursued.

In contrast to Rawls (and Taylor), Robert Nozick presents an alternative viewpoint which we can contrast with the "Theory of Justice".

Nozick & liberty

In *Anarchy, State and Utopia*, Nozick (1974) presents his view that *a priori*, the rights of the individual are paramount. The individual has rights that are inviolable by either other individuals or the state, they have ownership (property rights) over themselves in the same way that they have ownership over inanimate objects; therefore, inviolable right of control or transfer over themselves and their assets. Like Plato before him, Nozick tests his ideas to destruction. Where Plato tests the idea of meritocracy, showing us what is necessary to truly have this, Nozick shows what necessarily happens if individual liberty is prized above all else.

This position leads Nozick to state that there is no such thing as the "public good" (in contrast to both Bentham and Rawls), only benefits or disbenefits accrued to the individual; Nozick puts it thus,

> there is no **social entity** with a good that undergoes some sacrifice for its own good. There are only individual people, different individual people, with their own individual lives. Using one of these people for

the benefit of others, uses him and benefits the others. Nothing more. What happens is that something is done to him for the sake of others. Talk of an overall social good covers this up. (Intentionally?) To use a person in this way does not sufficiently respect and take account of the fact that he is a separate person, that his is the only life he has. **He** does not get some over-balancing good from his sacrifice, and no one is entitled to force this upon him – least of all a state or government that claims his allegiance (as other individuals do not) and that therefore scrupulously must be **neutral** between its citizens.

(Nozick, 1974, pp. 32–33 [author's emphasis])

Ownership looms large in Nozick's writing (Wolff, 1991). Nozick's view that the individual has inviolable rights (sovereignty) over himself and his property and his belief that government should be neutral leads him to assert that state action to benefit one individual at the cost of another is unacceptable. This is a use of the second formulation of Kant's Categorical Imperative (Kant, 1997) that an individual must only ever be treated as an end in themselves and never a means to the ends of others. One cannot formulate some utopian end state where one person's resources are commandeered for the benefit of another (King, 2011).

Instead, Nozick asserts that it is the legitimacy of exchange that matters; where an individual accrues assets by a fair means of exchange, he has an inviolable right to use or dispose of these assets as he pleases. Where the accrual of assets has not been via "fair" means, Nozick finds that it is a legitimate role of the (minimal) state to mediate and order reparations thus in the case of the trans-Atlantic slave trade for example, there are accruals to some individuals that are the result of unfair (to say the least) practices (outside fair contracts or exchange). Slavery of course also first violates the second formulation of the categorical imperative (as above) and another Nozickian concept, "side-constraints". This concept states that individual freedom is inviolable only up to the point that it infringes on that of another; best explained by the famous maxim *"My right to swing my fist stops where your face begins!"* So, for Nozick individual rights of property (including mastery over oneself) are inviolable but only to the point that first, one cannot use another as means to any end, and second that the sovereignty of others isn't violated (in this he agrees with Locke). In these, and only these, circumstances intervention by the state is justifiable to right the wrong and provide reparations (compensation).

Rawls and Nozick provide two very different conceptions of justice and therefore the role of the state in relation to the individual. Rawls' is based on the "fairness" of outcome. He accepts that inequality exists but also insists that the poorest must be as well off as they can be for this to be perceived as just. The state's intervention to ensure this is the case is entirely justified for Rawls, for example, the taxation of the wealthy to redistribute wealth to the poor is desirable, even essential for Rawls – even though it entails using some people and a means to the end of fairness. For Nozick (and Kant), this is completely unacceptable. Taxation and redistribution in this way violates the sovereignty of the self (and property), uses some as a means to the ends of others and violates the concept of side-constraints. The use of force must be permitted to enforce the removal of property from another.

The post-war consensus or first way

Following a second great war, pressure built for a new social deal. With roots in the Marxist and Fabian socialist traditions (Foord & Simic, 2005), the post-war consensus (as it became known) and related housing policies can broadly be said to be in the "social democratic" tradition. The post-war "social democracy" had equality at its heart (Crossland, 1956; Plant, 1996). It sought to harness the economic growth produced in a mixed (public and private) economy with social policies designed to produce greater equality; both of opportunity and outcome. In doing this social democracy provides a mid-ground between democratic and radical socialism (Jay, 1986) acknowledging that the homogeneous, capital-owning class predicted by Marx had not come about.

To implement this, more equal, vision of society based upon incremental growth and Keynesian economic management (see Keynes, 1936), the government took control of the means of production for those things most closely related to the provision of infrastructure. In terms of housing, health, welfare and education, citizens were no longer subject to market forces and held a stake in society via the non-capitalist (nationalised) industries and systems that recognised "need" as a variable that should play a role in the allocation of resources rather than allocation by market forces (see Plant, 1996).

Even in the period after World War 2 where the Atlee government embarked upon the setup of a huge bureaucracy designed to provide cradle-to-grave healthcare to all, free at the point of need (see Baggott, 2004; Dean, 2008; Hill, 1996; Lavalette & Pratt, 2009) vulnerable people found themselves forgotten. Despite progress in other areas, e.g. housing and health, the lot of those needing care and support barely improved. Permissions were granted to local authorities to provide services, but these were largely ignored (Irving-Clarke, 2016; Means et al., 2008).

Goodwin (1990) also notes that increases in funding were not proportional, using the term "Cinderella services". In the early 1950s, funding for services was 20% of the health budget despite mental deficiency hospitals having 40% of the patients. Martin (1995) states that large-scale hospitals were poorly run and ran restrictive regimes. They housed around 1,500 people with varying diagnoses. In response to the "Domesday book of hospital services", a government survey of hospital provision, the government produced the *National Assistance Act 1948* (Means et al., 2008). Aside from the provision of home care, the 1948 Act made little difference to the lives of the vulnerable. Both Parker (1965) and Eyden (1965) were scathing in their criticisms (Irving-Clarke, 2016). Over the next 30 years, piecemeal legislation added to the responsibilities of local authorities, the Hospital Plan 1962 planned and executed the closure of large-scale institutions, but as Murphy (1991) notes, community services for the vulnerable were not forthcoming; Murphy calls the years between 1962 and 1990 the "*disaster years*".

Given the grand plans of the post-war consensus to build a grand "social democracy", the massive investment in council housing, NHS and the nationalisation of key industries, the treatment of the vulnerable could not be more counter to these lofty goals. This was also reflected in the lot of people who found themselves homeless. Provision for them was largely in the form of large, communal dormitory accommodation known as "spikes" and was largely associated with middle-aged men with drinking problems. The first duties to assist homeless people were not enacted until 1977.

Thatcher, new public management and the second way

The election of Margaret Thatcher as Prime Minister in 1979 brought the end of the post-war consensus of Keynesian economic management and nationalised industries. Thatcher brought the monetarist theories of Milton Friedman (amongst others) to the political mainstream. Monetarist thinkers believed that public servants (and others) were motivated to act by their own self-interest and that "public interest" or its wider ideology is a fallacy; the only true democracy being that of the market. Therefore, the use of a quasi-market mechanism to procure and manage public services could be used to ensure that public sector managers focused on the needs of consumers rather than themselves. Public choice theory developed as the underpinning idea behind Thatcher's new polity.

This theory relied on two key drivers; first, the consumer acting selfishly to fulfil their own needs/desires and exercising choice between services thus driving the "market". The second driver would be created by government imposing requirements and targets upon officials, thus driving them to act in their own self-interest in fulfilling these targets. As Seddon (2008) puts it,

Public sector managers have a surrogate profit motive, a target that defines success, and the incentive to earn investment in their organisation and recognition among their peers.

(p. 7)

The "public choice" school paved the way for reform to public services across the world and especially the UK; Margaret Thatcher was one of the key protagonists of the theory (Savage & Atkinson, 2001). Savage and Atkinson draw a direct line between public choice theory and the emergence of "New Public Management" (NPM) in the UK from 1979 to the present. (The term New Public Management was coined by Christopher Pollitt in 1990.)

NPM was distinguishable from public administration in several key respects, first, and perhaps most importantly, it moved away from the thus far dominant ideas of Weberian bureaucracy where there is seen to be a direct line of accountability between elected politicians and their civil servants. The implementation process in the traditional model was governed by established rules and procedures that clearly separate personal interests from those of the role of the civil servant.

NPM pays greater attention to results or outputs and the personal responsibility of individual managers (from Hughes, 1998), it emphasises a move from tall hierarchies to flatter, more flexible and devolved management structures with more flexible terms of employment (from Horton & Farnham, 1999). Institutional and individual objectives are clearly defined and include the establishment of key performance indicators (KPIs) against which to measure delivered outputs (Horton & Farnham 1999; Hughes, 1998). There is greater attention to economy, efficiency and effectiveness as greater commitment to procedures such as market testing and compulsory competitive tendering (Elcock, 1991; Hughes, 1998). Finally, there is a general commitment to reducing the role of the state in the disposal of gross national product and the provision of services in favour of privatised companies and the establishment of a market in areas previously viewed as the preserve of natural monopolies or public administrators (Hughes, 1998). This generally meant the nationalised industries mentioned in the previous section.

These concepts are important here, the implementation of Supported Housing policy very clearly shows the intention to move Local Authorities from the role of provider of services to that of commissioner. The *NHS and Community Care Act 1990* restructured Social Services with local authorities moving from being direct providers of services to commissioners. Social services (e.g. personal care) were provided by private or semi-private companies with a focus on competition at the commissioning stage with these organisations "tendering" to provide services on behalf of the authority.

The Supporting People policy moved local authorities to this approach. Whilst the changes of 1990 were those of a Conservative government, the New Labour government elected in 1997 very clearly embraced these ideas under Blair and Brown (including in relation to the provision of support). Their distinct approach is outlined in the following section.

New Labour and the third way

The New Labour governments of Blair and Brown followed a neo-liberal agenda in some regards, retaining a focus upon the global economy, reform of the welfare state, a drive for modernisation and a focus upon targets, indicators and audit and inspection regimes (Newman 2001; Seddon, 2008). However, Newman (2001) shows a more complex reality in that the (New) Labour governments "*...attempted to establish – and sustain – a new set of political alliances. It sought to forge a consensus around an agenda of 'modernising' reforms designed to remedy deep-seated social problems...*" (p. 1). Newman also found a softening of the ideological commitment to market mechanisms and competition as drivers of public sector reform. There was emphasis upon innovation, experimentation and policy evaluation in public services backed by a commitment to evidence-based policy in many areas (Nutley et al., 2007).

Labour's modernisation agenda went beyond mere economics however. There was a reimagining of the cultural and social spheres. New Labour saw themselves as having to reconcile retention of the economic gains of the Thatcher governments with a reshaping of civil society via the invocation of moral and civic values and a new emphasis on citizenship and social inclusion. They also sought to appeal to new groups, women, black and minority ethnic communities, disabled people, LGBT groups and the young. These were groups that they (New Labour) saw as excluded from the political system. At the same time, they sought to play down class-based enmity – a corollary of "Old Labour" (Newman, 2001). Newman (2014) also identified that women were expected to become "full worker-citizens" (p. 442) and that previous feminist framings of "welfare" had also been partially displaced.

The Third Way can be defined against the two prevailing ideologies of the 20th century. The First Way of the "old left" emphasised Keynesian management of the economy that favoured the agencies of the state to accomplish social policy goals whilst also acknowledging the role of the private sector in a mixed economy. The Second Way was that of the New Right, embodied by the Thatcher and Major governments of the 1970s and 1980s. The New Right favoured a laissez-faire approach to the economy, finding free-market solutions to all problems, placed emphasis on economic individualism and prizing personal economic gain over social issues and values (Driver & Martell, 1999).

The Institute for Public Policy Research (IPPR, 1994) provided much of the intellectual ballast for the third-way project. The Commission for Social Justice identified investment as the way out of the country's maladies. The report suggests investing in the population by encouraging and facilitating lifelong learning. Opportunity is clearly conceptualised as, if not synonymised with, working for a living. The state can promote this via providing learning opportunities, promoting equality by minimising segregation between "men's" and "women's" jobs and promoting family-friendly work environments. Alongside this is the proposal to build an intelligent welfare state that prevents and alleviates poverty, protects people from the risks of a changing labour market and redistributes resources across the life cycle, both encouraging independence and promoting social cohesion.

The Third Way embodied both previous systems, promoting social justice, the market and community. It could embrace market enterprise but not automatically favour market solutions, promote a positive role for the state but not assume the state should provide services directly, and offer a communitarian view of society rather than an individualistic one. Blair's position was that the Third Way represented a modern social democracy, a path on the centre left of politics and an opportunity to advance centre-left values whilst utilising policies that were suited to the modern world. Blair's view was therefore that the Third Way was not a path between left and right (a middle way) or between the First and Second Ways, but a new strand on the left.

A timely point to make about the Third Way here, is the thought that it is light on ideology and heavy on pragmatism (unlike its first- and second-way predecessors). It was values that mattered to the Third Way project rather than separate policies or how they are delivered. Blair (1998) outlines these values as equal worth, opportunity for all, responsibility (correlated with rights) and community. The Third Way is not tied to the state (First Way) or the market (second way) as mechanisms of delivery, but rather seeks to work with the voluntary sector, government (local and national) and other agencies so solve the complex social problems that government faces (Driver & Martell, 1999). A key early influence on Tony Blair, Amitai Etzioni (1994, 1997, 1998) promoted (and continues to promote) communitarianism as the preferable way to organise society and redistribute resources. Communitarians reject the liberal individualism of the political and economic right in favour of an approach which favours social solidarity and social cohesion (Watts & Fitzpatrick, 2018). All members of a given social group have an interest and duty in ensuring the well-being of others in the group. The duty exists outside of any "social contract" between individual and state but can be fulfilled by state action. Communitarians' main concern is with minimising social exclusion (Watts & Fitzpatrick, 2018). Gray (2000) goes so far as to say that the wealthy hold no duty to those less so other than the provision of fair opportunities and basic needs – beyond this, distribution is not an issue.

Like Etzioni (and Communitarians more generally), Giddens (1998) asks questions about the implications of the supposed individualism that exists and the implications for social solidarity (that had been a mainstay of social democracy). What exactly is the new individualism and how does it relate to the increasing role of markets? His concern is that society is becoming "me-first" and that this is destroying common values and public concerns. He is clear that social democrats should preserve a core concern with social justice whilst accepting that the range of issues that divide left from right is shrinking. Where equality was seen to conflict with individual autonomy, Giddens suggests that new relationships between the individual and society must be forged. He distils these down into two basic maxims, *"no rights without responsibility"* and *"no authority without democracy"*. This is reflected in the contractual arrangements between local authorities and providers for services and agreements between service providers and service users.

The first of these *"no rights without responsibility"* is intended to replace the model that sees rights as unconditional. Where Locke sees that there are rights that are ours as a result of merely being human, life, liberty and the pursuit of happiness (as in the US constitution), the role of the state is to preserve these rights and ensure they are not infringed upon; Giddens finds that decreasing social solidarity and increasing individualism demands a new contract. He proposes that rights can only be granted where corresponding responsibilities also adhered to. He is also clear that such conditionality must apply to all in society, not only those in need of state assistance (as the right often propose).

Second, Giddens proposes that there should be *"no authority without democracy"*. This is in direct contravention of right-wing ideology; the right has always looked at tradition as a means of conferring authority on institutions, e.g. the church, family or state; and without due deference to these institutions, authority crumbles. Giddens argues that increasing individualism and decreasing faith in and attention to custom and tradition mean that (again) a new social agreement is required – one where the sole source of establishing authority is via democracy. Using these precepts, Giddens outlines his vision of the "social investment state".

The social investment state

Giddens is critical of the neo-liberal conception of society as a meritocracy, one where the conception of equality is that of equality of opportunity. As far as he is concerned, this concept of equality leads to unacceptable inequalities and some people and groups receiving rewards that are dispro-portionate to their talents or contributions. He argues that this inequality leads to some groups in society becoming dislocated from the rest, at the top and the bottom. Extreme wealth at the top could allow a group of "un-touchables" to pull away from society and choose to withdraw from social institutions. At the bottom, the very poor are rendered unable to partici-pate in civil society because of lack of resources.

Le Grand (1999) is also critical of Conservative policies that consider it enough to attempt to create a "level playing field" and is supportive of government intervention to redistribute resources in favour of those that require additional support and training. The Third Way concep-tion of this is not based upon the Marxist ideas of exploitation of the working classes by the bourgeoisie but rather a refusal to accept this as an excuse for failure. Le Grand emphasises the importance of personal responsibility in breaking the cycle of deprivation. He gives the example of government investment being matched by personal effort – schools will be improved by investment, but the individual has a responsibility to ensure that they and their children take advantage of this by attending and working hard.

The Third Way conception of equality is as "*equality as inclusion*" and this is the key to the Third Way conception of the relationship between the individual and the state. In Giddens' view, the ability of the super-rich to pull away at the top of society and the poor's inability to fully participate in society are just as damaging as one another. Giddens outlines how the majority of income gains in the US over the last 30 years have gone to the top 1%, whilst the income of the poorest 25% has remained static or de-clined over the same period. The trend in the UK is less severe but along the same pattern.

Giddens accepts the need to reform welfare provision but advocates strongly for its existence as a redistributory mechanism. This meant that the institutions of government, the voluntary sector and individuals must be set up to cooperate rather than compete (as they had been under Thatcherism). The drive for inclusion was to come from reinvigorated and empowered communities, hence Labour's enthusiasm for devolving power to Scotland, Wales and the London Authority.

His argument is that where welfare systems benefit most of the people liv-ing in a society, this fosters a "*common morality of citizenship*" (p. 108), whereas when there is a purely negative connotation of welfare, this is divisive. For Giddens, leaving people reliant on benefits isolates them from broader so-ciety and removing benefits to force people into work (conditionality) forces them into an already-overcrowded, low-skilled labour market. Le Grand (1999) enforces this view that the "exploited class" are in fact now exploited by the systems set up to help them; trapped on benefits and let down by a failing education system and NHS.

In this regard, Third Way policy has a strong moral vein, relating back to the communitarian influence of Etzioni. The individual has a responsibility not only to themselves but also to the community. For example, jobseekers were required to show they were looking for work in exchange for receiving financial support from the state; in exchange for improved education and schools, parents have a responsibility to ensure homework is being done. The government promised to crack down on absent parents who were shirking their responsibilities. In these areas and more the Third Way sees the relationship between the individual and the state as one of reciprocity, the state will support you in your ambitions, but the onus is on you to work hard and earn your reward. For the Third Way, education and skills are the way to encourage inclusion in the labour market and therefore raise the incomes and self-esteem of those who would otherwise be marginalised by the lack of these.

Likewise, hospitals and the health service would be invested in and improved, but this was matched by an expectation that the individual would take responsibility for looking after their own health, e.g. giving up smoking. As part of this theme, there is a determination also that work is not only the best route out of poverty but is also the source of self-worth; therefore, training and services will be provided, but it is the responsibility of the individual to take these up. This does leave open the question of what should happen to those who do not take up the mantle of these responsibilities.

In summary then, at its core the Third Way is an attempt to transform governance to meet the changing demands of the modern world; to govern in a globalised world where social movements are based upon common cause across socio-economic boundaries that risk old style socialism/social democracy becoming obsolete. To fashion a new social contract between the state and individual that recognises the individual whilst supporting communities, that confers rights but also responsibilities.

Criticisms of the Third Way

As one might expect, the Third Way has not been without its critics. Chief amongst these is that the Third Way is little more than pragmatism rather than ideology. Second, it has been asked whether the Third Way is really a radical programme of renewal or a clever marketing gimmick for a continuation of Thatcherism (King, 2001) – global capitalism with a human face.

King also highlights the neo-Marxist philosopher Slavoj Žižek's objections to the Third Way. In Žižek's view the Third Way is little more than a tacit admission that there is actually *"no alternative to the Second Way, no actual alternative to global capitalism*" (Žižek, 2000, pp. 62–63) and it is precisely the lack of ideology in the Third Way that allows for the maintenance of the liberal global elite.

Žižek is also critical of the Third Way for its pragmatism. In his view, the Third Way is an attempt to forge a politics without enemies, a politics with whom no one can disagree. This he sees as a mistake, in his view, in its pragmatism of trying to please everyone; the Third Way will become the politics of identity and grievance. This is an error in his view as it prevents a truly universal politics emerging to challenge global capital. Stressing difference and otherness can only serve to alienate any use of the universal – as a Marxist, Žižek sees the main struggle of the proletariat as being a primarily economic one and therefore any splits in the proletariat along anything other than the economic grounds diminish the possibility of a Marxist revolution. This has relevance for Supporting People and welfare policy more generally as will be discussed later.

If the Third Way is little more than pragmatism and a politics without enemies, it is also open to the criticism that it is not particularly realistic. And this was thrown into sharp relief on September 11, 2001. King (2001) described the Blair/Clinton approach as the politics of survival and little else, their goal being not to upset anyone so much that it cost them their grip on power. The attack on the twin towers ended this approach; as King sees it, in the face of such an event political survival necessitated an absolute response. The Third Way of compromise was of little use in this arena, if we accept King's premise then we accept that there are times where political survival (if that is the goal) cannot only dependent on the politics of pragmatism and compromise.

Giddens himself acknowledges many of the criticisms of Third Way thinking and indeed published a second book *The Third Way and Its Critics* (Giddens, 2001) in which he summarises what he sees as the main criticisms. These are as follows.

First, that the Third Way is essentially an amorphous political project, incapable of being properly defined. Giddens sees this as a function of a point I have already made, namely that the Third Way is defined largely in terms of what it is not, rather than what it is, and this renders it without active definition. The First Way of social democracy and Second Way of neo-liberalism are fully formed and thus can respond more effectively to the political challenges they face.

Second, it fails to sustain a left-wing outlook and whether purposely or not, lapses into conservatism. This criticism is advancing the view, that we have already heard, that rather than being something radical or new, the left has simply moved the right on a number issues. Thus, mirroring Žižek's criticism of the Third Way as merely the continuation of right-wing economic hegemony; an admission that there is no Third Way, indeed no alternative to the Second Way at all. Giddens quotes Stuart Hall's criticism that New Labour are far too preoccupied with middle England, middle class voters in the south and have forsaken their heartland of manual workers in the north of the country as evidence of this.

Third, and in a related point, there is a criticism that the Third Way merely accepts the basic neo-liberal framework. Globalisation is seen as a given and most importantly the Third Way fails to contest the inequalities of wealth and power that neo-liberalism produces. In short, Giddens states that the Third Way offers nothing to the losers of globalisation as it has adopted the narrative of the winners. This has been seen most recently through the prism of the "Brexit" vote where socio-economic and socio-cultural class played a major role. In wanting to limit the size of the state, the scope of the state to redistribute wealth (a major preoccupation of social democrats) has also been limited.

Fourth, the Third Way is a primarily Anglo-Saxon creation with the hallmarks of those societies. Whilst it is of some use in countries with less developed welfare systems (I assume Giddens is comparing the UK with the Scandinavian economies here), it has little application in those countries with more evolved welfare provision.

Fifth, the Third Way has no distinctive economic strategy other than allowing the market to rule. Both the First Way and Second Way have distinctive and well-developed economic strategies based on state intervention and market privatisation and deregulation, respectively. The Third Way provides no such clarity and as such is prone to drift. Giddens quotes Alan Ryan's (p. 25) prescient criticism that the Third Way has merely been riding the crest of economic prosperity and has no solution should there be a downturn.

I do not intend to rehearse Giddens' arguments against these criticisms here; if you are interested you only need pick up a copy of his own book. But where these will be important are later when I come to look at Supporting People and welfare policy more widely in relation to the Third Way. What has been covered above are both the issues that Third Way policy was intended to address and the criticisms of the Third Way as a guiding philosophy for social policy. Chapter 4 will look in detail at both the development of welfare policy through the first and Second Ways and then specifically at the Supporting People programme as the keystone of New Labour's approach to supporting vulnerable people.

Ideology, philosophy and supported housing

There has been a long-term failure to provide adequate services for poor and vulnerable people. Houses of Industry/Correction, the workhouse, asylums and inadequate community services have failed to provide care and support to those the policies were designed to help. These policies have failed both on their own terms (see McConnell's framework) and implementation of them has been bedevilled by administrators not taking seriously the intentions of policymakers – often when they are patently clear.

But what of the philosophical tests for policy? Earlier in this chapter, I have laid out the ideological frameworks that have underpinned government policy for much of the time that supported housing has existed; from the classical liberal ideas that led to the workhouse and asylums (designed to take the disruptive out of the workforce), the social democratic ideas of the post-war period, Thatcherite policies of the 1980s and 1990s and Third Way of Blair and Brown. Throughout this time, there has been an inexorable march from the paternalistic, generic environments of asylums to more individualistic treatments and services. Early policy treated all paupers in the same way, regardless of the causes of their condition, age or disability. Over time, the law has recognised that there are different groups of people that require different treatments and support. This has culminated in the recognition of a wide range of different groups that require support.

My contention at the start of this chapter was that supported housing provides a good proxy for the relationship between individual and state. Early interventions in the "liberal" era were aimed at punishing the poor for their lack of means. Whether the stocks, the workhouse or the asylum, the clear aim was to incentivise people against being in such a situation. The state at this time was highly paternalistic, acting to ensure individuals behaved in an acceptable way for their own good. The divine right of kings saw the monarch as the figurative "parent" of all citizens and the state acted accordingly.

The workhouse and asylums particularly reflect this, but also reflect the effect of the bureaucratic state. This developed during the 18th century as the government began to tax its citizens to pay for a state apparatus. These institutions reflect the stereotypical state bureaucracy with people being treated as part of generic groups, individuality lost in the system. Even in the post-war social democratic system of the welfare state people in need of support from the state were not taken care of adequately. Local authorities were granted permissions to provide services that they did not use, duties were not conferred except in some rare cases. Large-scale hospitals replaced the asylums, Erving Goffman's work on "total institutions" and evaluations from Eyden and others reflected the harsh reality of these institutions. Some of the reasons for inaction are given in Chapter 4.

The reforms to community care made in 1990 gave some hope, with local authorities transformed into commissioners of care and away from direct provision. But again, these changes were bedevilled by inadequate leadership, inadequate funding and bureaucracy. Also, at this time, many of the large-scale hospitals were closed in favour of smaller community-based care homes and support services.

New Labour's third-way project was exemplified by the Supporting People programme. Their focus on social investment reflected in the ring-fenced funding and focus upon service user involvement in services. Supporting documents (e.g. DETR, 2001) make special reference to the involvement of older people and black and minority ethnic (BME) communities; the programme also reflected Third Way ideas about rights and responsibilities. Investment in services was provided on the condition that those using the services participated in contractual agreements to work to address their issues, although there was criticism that Supporting People stopped short of giving people "rights" to services and this made insisting on services (or enforcing rights) problematic (see Audit Commission 2005, 2009; Irving-Clarke, 2016). The Third Way saw equality as inclusion and much of the framework around Supporting People reflected this belief in inclusion in civic life as a merit good – a good thing in its own right.

Rawls, Nozick and supported housing

In the social contract (considered above) it is made clear that such a contract exists. Whether one believes Hobbes or Locke as regards the state of nature, groups of people have come together and formed a "state" giving up some of their rights to a central sovereign authority in return for both protection and the judicial resolution of disputes. The question we are left with then, is have people in need of support been treated justly?

Above I set out two tests (of several) to test this. I will start with Nozick. Nozick emphasises the primacy of contractual exchanges in fairly allocating property. The individual has the right to do with his property (this includes himself) as he wishes, as long as it does not impinge upon the rights of others (what Nozick calls "side constraints"). In addition, people are to be treated as "ends" in themselves and never as a means to ends of others. The (minimal) state must also act to correct situations where current ownership has come about because of past injustices, reparations for the trans-Atlantic slave trade or holocaust would be two examples where this has happened.

One of the advantages Nozick claims for his system is that it takes historic account of ownership and transfer in a way that theorists such as Rawls do not. Rawls is merely concerned with the distribution of resources in the present and how this can be made just. One of the problems for Nozick (and us) here is that the policies we are talking about stretch back to the 15th century. There may yet be a case that many of those who own property in the present had ancestors that came by it unjustly and those who find themselves disenfranchised lost out unfairly at some point in the distant past. Our problem here is that records of how resources came to be distributed have long since passed into antiquity and to a large degree, we are where we are. However, that is not to say that Nozick is of no use to us.

If we look at the history of provision of support it is clear that if, as Nozick does, one believes in the primacy of exchange then those with few resources are treated justly if those who do own the resources came by them through fair and just exchange. However, Nozick also prizes the sovereignty of the individual highly. The placing of people in the stocks for no other crime than being poor is in clear contravention of personal sovereignty. Where an individual, however poor, has not impinged upon the rights of others, the state has no right to impinge upon their rights. Hobbes and Locke would surely agree that merely being poor is no reason for your rights to be infringed upon or removed. Likewise, if we look at Houses of Correction or Industry or the workhouse, Nozick would also find these unacceptable. Enforced servitude in such a place in return for the most meagre board and lodgings would sure be considered using people as a means to the end of the state, breaking both Nozick's and Kant's rules in this regard.

Asylums too are considered unacceptable. The incarceration of people in "total institutions" locked away from the rest of society on highly suspect grounds (in many cases) and with little in the way of due process violates individual rights. Whilst asylums might fulfil their policy goal and purpose of keeping disruptive people out of the workhouse or workplace, Nozick (and Locke) would surely consider them a gross infringement on the rights of the individual. Hobbes may, of course, dissent from this view. His contention that a Leviathan state is preferable to living in the state of nature leads him to conclude that the workhouse or asylum is an acceptable infringement to protect those incarcerated and wider social principles. One example of this is the detention of people considered "moral imbeciles"; this included women who had children outside marriage and those considered sexually promiscuous.

More recent innovations such as the Supporting People programme and services provided by social care departments may find more approval from Nozick as they are, in the main, voluntary and only require compulsion where a court finds this necessary. However, the provision of such services by the state requires funding raised via taxation and this is something that Nozick finds to be unacceptable, treating taxpayers and means to the ends of the state and others and therefore, not to be tolerated. As I pointed out earlier, Nozick's theory is largely an exercise in abstract thought about what the world would be like if we prized the liberty of the individual above all else. Whilst it provides a framework through which we can protect the rights of the individual from being incarcerated unfairly, it is not practical in a world where a social contract exists, and the state requires funding to fulfil the requirements of such a contract. Perhaps then, we can turn to Rawls', or Taylor's modified framework for help?

Rawls' original framework addresses the distribution of wealth in society stating that inequality is only acceptable if it means that the worst off in society are in as good a position as possible. Rawls also provides a test, the difference principle, that allows us to conceptualise how we might decide what a just society looks like. This test places us behind a "veil of ignorance" and decides what a just society might look like. One of the problems with this test is that it assumes that once knowledge about one's own circumstances are removed, we will act in a munificent fashion and design a system in which all receive adequate support – this, however, is not a given.

Taylor (2018) in her revised framework replaces material goods with the ability of the individual to come to their own perception of a good life and the ability to be able to pursue that conception. Given that the purpose of supported housing is to provide people with the care and support they need to participate in society, Taylor's test is the better for our purpose; indeed, if we combine it with the Third Way conception of equality as inclusion in civic life, it becomes a powerful tool with which to assess policy.

Prior to the setting up of the welfare state following World War 2, and as we have discussed at some length in Chapter 4, paupers were put into the workhouse where they had to work in order to pay for their upkeep, in asylums or large-scale hospitals where they were often incarcerated for many years with little to no due process or otherwise left to beg on the streets. It does not take a huge leap of the mind to see that all these policies fail both Rawls' original test and Taylor's modified version. The distribution of wealth was such that the poor were very far from as well off as they could be, levels of wealth inequality were huge. Also, social change at this time (caused by the industrial revolution) meant that many people left rural areas for employment in cities causing breakdown of traditional support structures, people with disabilities were excluded from the workplace as machinery was designed to be operated by the able-bodied.

Policy at this time also fails Taylor's modified test. For similar reasons, she discusses with reference to the "Bedroom Tax", lack of financial and other provision for paupers meant that they expended much of their existence just surviving so that they had little time or resource to expend upon conceiving what a "good life" meant for them, let alone have the ability to pursue it. Likewise, incarceration in faceless institutions such as asylums or large hospitals, whether brutal, neglectful or both, allowed no opportunity to do this. As Goffman's (1970) work on "total institutions" says, individuals become institutionalised and eventually unable to live outside the institution, so inculcated are they with the routines of the institution.

Following World War 2, there was a step change in welfare provision. The setting up of the NHS, comprehensive education and welfare state, including a massive housing building programme, aimed to provide cradle-to-grave support to everyone in the population. Financial means would no longer be a barrier to receive healthcare, education or decent housing. The provision of care and support to the vulnerable did not follow the same path. Good intentions were followed by poor implementation. Despite a plethora of legislation granting local authorities' permissions to set up community-based services, large-scale institutions remained the norm, especially for the chronically sick, including the elderly (Irving-Clarke, 2016). As discussed previously, services for vulnerable people remained of low status attracting disproportionately lower funding levels and remaining a low-status career route for professionals (Murphy, 1991). Murphy dubs the years between 1962 and 1990 "*the disaster years*". The social democratic principles set out above were not extended to people needing care and support.

Policy in this period cannot therefore be said to meet Taylor's test. The continuing detention of the vulnerable in large-scale institutions is inconsistent with the aim of allowing them to conceptualise and pursue their version of a good life.

The *NHS and Community Care Act 1990* had the potential to provide real change for vulnerable people. Local authorities were transformed from providers to commissioners of services with some success and could now commission services from the voluntary and private sectors. These sectors expanded to accommodate the demand. Means et al. (2008) note that there was some success in allowing frail elderly people to access services in their own homes rather than relying on residential care and younger disabled people were able to access a range of services via direct payments. However, Means et al. (*ibid*) are critical of the funding provided to provide such services noting that local authorities routinely spent more than their allocation of funds. Rummery (2002) found that the role of care managers as gatekeepers to funding made it difficult for them to both limit spending and promote individual choice and self-determination (as per Taylor's test). Lewis and Glennerster (1996) state that local authorities responded to these new challenges with bureaucracy, concentrating on implementing structures rather than listening to practitioners and service users. Baggott (2004) notes the high cost of commissioning and poor relationships between commissioners and providers. Once again, this points towards a dysfunctional system that does not allow service users to pursue a self-determined vision of a good life, indeed Rummery (2002) as much as says so.

Another innovation of the Thatcher governments were the changes to legislation around homelessness. Until the National Assistance Act 1948 accommodation for homeless people had mostly been in "spikes", (large poor-quality dormitories) often converted workhouses; these were largely associated with middle-aged "men of the road" (Neale, 1997). The *Housing Act 1996* placed new duties on local authorities to secure interim accommodation for those deemed vulnerable under the act and permanent accommodation thereafter if investigation revealed they fell within one of the "vulnerable" categories specified. These "vulnerable" groups were extended by the *Homelessness Act 2002*. One important qualification was that in addition to being deemed vulnerable, you must not have made yourself "intentionally homeless" by giving up accommodation or having been evicted for rent arrears or another breach of tenancy.

These policy changes also fail Taylor's test. First, the changes led to local authorities having to create strategic housing departments to take on housing duties from social services departments and this meant creating a division between those who did not meet the threshold for social care, but still required support to live independently (Irving-Clarke, 2016). Many people fell through the gap created. The duty placed upon authorities was the provision of housing, the duty to provide such support so as to enable people to maintain housing remained lacking. This led to tenancy failure and repeat homelessness (*ibid*). In addition, people without a local connection to the local authority in question or those who were deemed to have caused their own homelessness were also expressly excluded from the housing duty (in an echo of earlier conditionality). In other words, there were a considerable number of people that either fell through the gaps or had no right to services.

The Third Way and supporting people

New Labour's "Third Way" supported housing policy "Supporting People" again offered hope for vulnerable people. The programme also went some way to beginning to meet Taylor's test. Audit Commission (2005, 2009), Fyson et al. (2007) and Communities and Local Government (CLG) Committee (2009) highlighted the successes of the programme. Partnerships between mainstream health, social care, housing budgets were managed well in some areas; often associated with the better performing authorities. Existing services had been remodelled reducing costs, better meeting local needs and linking services more effectively; services not delivering acceptable quality, decommissioned or improved. Innovative approaches to service delivery had been encouraged and secured (Audit Commission, 2005).

Outcomes for service users improved, greater user involvement, choice and control were noted as important factors (Audit Commission, 2009). The new outcomes framework and requirements to measure and record had made providers think in a more service user centred way. More localised services had made access easier for many groups. CLG guidance on removing local connection policies (not a requirement) had also meant that some authorities had taken a less *"parochial attitude"* (Audit Commission [2009], p. 18).

There had also been a move from more paternalistic approaches to services in some areas. The *"...culture of inclusiveness, partnership working and consultation..."* (Audit Commission, 2009, p. 19) within the programme is credited with this. Examples are given where service users and ex-service users have acted as peer reviewers. There is also a suggestion that use of service users in procurement has led to improvements in value for money (VFM) and outcomes.

Local and national governance arrangements enabled a structured framework to involve service users and providers. The quality assessment framework and performance monitoring system enabled consistent benchmarking across providers and service areas and empowered local administration to monitor and improve value for money and challenge poor performers to improve. In addition, the ring-fenced grant allowed reinvestment of savings into new services.

Some of the successes of the programme were that it had allowed more independent living and can be cost-effective and contribute to desired policy outcomes across virtually all service user groups. Despite some criticisms, there were improvements in the focus on service users and carers, attention on value for money, improvements to the range and quality of services, new impetus to dealing with some long-standing issues and improved local partnership working. However, the programme stopped short of imposing duties upon local authorities to provide services and did not provide redress to people to enforce their rights to services to enable them to live independently, and therefore, unable to self-determine a conception of a good life. The removal of the funding ring-fence in 2010 combined with the impact of the financial crisis in 2008 conspired to remove large amounts of funding from the programme, it is now all but non-existent. The gains were short-lived.

Chapter 4 gives a detailed account of the history of supported housing. This is currently at something of an impasse as we await policy proposals from the incumbent Conservative government. Their proposals for supported housing (now mostly abandoned) are covered in Chapter 4 also. Following that, Chapter 5 looks at the future of the sector and set out a potential blueprint for services.

References

Audit Commission (2005) *Supporting People*, Audit Commission, London.
Audit Commission (2009) *Supporting People*, Audit Commission, London.

Baggott, R (2004) *Health and Health Care in Britain* (3rd Edition), Palgrave MacMillan, Basingstoke.

Blair, T (1998) *The Third Way: New Politics for the New Century*, Fabian Society, London.

CLG Committee (2009) *The Supporting People Programme*, HMSO, London.

Crossland, CAR. (1956) *The Future of Socialism*, Constable & Robinson, London.

de Maistre, J (1996) *Against Rousseau: On the State of Nature and on the Sovereignty of People*, McGill-Queen's University Press, Montreal.

Dean, H (2008) *Social Policy*, Polity Press, Cambridge.

DETR (2001) *Supporting People: Policy into Practice*, HMSO, London.

Driver, S & Martell, L (1999) Left, right and the third way, *Policy and Politics* 28(2) pp. 147–461.

Elcock, H (1991) *Change and Decay? Public Administration in the 1990s*, Longman, Harlow.

Etzioni, A (1994) *The Politics of Community*, Fontana, London.

Etzioni, A (1997) *The New Golden Rule*, Profile Books, London.

Etzioni, A (ed) (1998) *The Essential Communitarian Reader*, Rowman & Littlefield, Oxford.

Eyden, J (1965) The physically handicapped in D Marsh (ed) *An Introduction to the Study of Social Administration*, Routledge and Kegan Paul, London pp. 161–174.

Filmer, R (1680) *Patriarcha: Of the Natural Power of Kings*, Richard Chiswell, London.

Foord, M & Simic, P (2005) *Housing, Community Care and Supported Housing – Resolving Contradictions*, CIH, Coventry.

Fyson, R et al. (2007) *Support for Living: The Impact of the Supporting People Programme on Housing and Support for Adults with Learning Disabilities*, Joseph Rowntree Foundation, New York.

Gibb, K (2015) The multiple policy failures of the Bedroom tax, *International Journal of Housing Policy* 15(2) pp. 148–166.

Giddens, A (1998) *The Third Way: The Renewal of Social Democracy*, Polity Press, Cambridge.

Giddens, A (2001) *The Third Way and its Critics*, Polity Press, Cambridge.

Godwin, W (1793) *Enquiry Concerning Political Justice*, G.G.J. and J. Robinson, London.

Goffman, E (1970) *Stigma: Notes on the Management of Spoiled Identity*, Penguin, London.

Goodin, RE (1993) Utility and the good in P Singer (ed) *A Companion to Ethics*, Blackwell, Oxford pp. 241–248.

Goodwin, S (1990) *Community Care and the Future of Mental Health Service Provision*, Avebury, Aldershot.

Gray, J (2000) Inclusion: A radical critique in P Askonas & A Stewart (eds) *Social Inclusion: Possibilities & Tensions*, MacMillan, Basingstoke pp. 19–36.

Hill (1996) *Social Policy: A Comparative Analysis*, TJ Press, Padstow.

Hobbes, T (1651) *Leviathan or The Matter, Forme and Power of a Common-Wealth Ecclesiastical and Civil*, London.

Horton, S & Farnham, D (1999) *Public Management in Britain*, Palgrave, Basingstoke.

Hughes, OE (1998) *Public Management and Administration*, MacMillan, London.

IPPR (1994) *Social Justice: Strategies for National Renewal, the Report of the Commission for Social Justice*, Vintage, London.

Irving-Clarke (2016) *Supporting People – How Did We Get Here and What Does It Mean for the Future?* Unpublished PhD thesis, De Montfort University, Leicester.

Jay, R (1986) Democracy in R Eccleshall et al. (eds) *Political Ideologies: An Introduction*, Hutchinson, London pp. 153–184.

Kant, I (1997) *Groundwork of the Metaphysics of Morals*, Cambridge University Press, Cambridge.

Keynes, JM (1936) *The General Theory of Employment, Interest and Money*, Palgrave MacMillan, London.

King, P (2001) Contemporary Housing Politics and the Politics of the Impossible: Žižek, Kant and the Third Way, Occasional Paper 71, De Montfort University, Leicester.

King, P (2011) *The Principles of Housing*, Routledge, London.

Kymlicka, W (2002) *Contemporary Political Philosophy: An Introduction*, Oxford University Press, Oxford.

Le Grand, J (1999) http://news.bbc.co.uk/1/hi/458626.stm, accessed November 25, 2018.

Lewis, J & Glennerster, H (1996) *Implementing the New Community Care*, Open University Press, Buckingham.

Locke, J (1690) *Two Treatises of Government*, Awnsham & Churchill, London.

Martin, M (1995) Medical knowledge and medical practice: Geriatric knowledge in the 1950s, *Social History of Medicine* 7(3) pp. 443–461.

Mead, L (1992) *The New Politics of Poverty*, Basic Books, New York.

Means, R et al. (2008) *Community Care* (4th Edition), Palgrave MacMillan, Basingstoke.

Moffatt, S et al. (2016) *A Qualitative Study of the Impact of the UK Bedroom Tax*, Oxford University Press, Oxford.

Murphy, E (1991) *After the Asylums: Community Care for People with Mental Illness*, Faber & Faber, London.

Neale, J (1997) Homelessness and Theory Reconsidered, *Housing Studies* 12(1) pp. 47–71.

Newman, J (2001) *New Labour, Policy and Society*, SAGE, London.

Newman, J (2014) Governing the Present: activism, neoliberalism and the problem of power and consent, *Critical Policy Studies* 8(2) pp. 133–147.

Nozick, R (1974) *Anarchy, State and Utopia*, Basic Books, New York.

Nutley, S et al. (2007) *Using Evidence: How Research Can Inform Public Services*, Policy Press, Bristol.

Parker, J (1965) *Local Health and Welfare Services*, Allen and Unwin, London.

Plant, R (1996) Social Democracy in D Marquand & A Seldon (eds), *The Ideas that Shaped Post war Britain*, Fontana, London pp. 165–194.

Plato (2007) *The Republic*, Penguin Books, London.

Rawls, J (1971) *A Theory of Justice*, Harvard University Press, Cambridge, MA, USA.

Rousseau, JJ (1762) *The Social Contract*, Paris.

Rummery, K (2002) *Disability, Citizenship & Community Care: A Case for Welfare Rights*, Ashgate, Aldershot.

Savage, R & Atkinson, S (2001) *Public Policy Under Blair*, Palgrave MacMillan, Basingstoke.

Scoccia, D (2008) In defense of hard paternalism, *Law and Philosophy* 27(4) pp. 351–381.

Seddon, J (2008) *Systems Thinking in the Public Sector*, Triarchy Press, Axminster.

Smart, JJC & Williams, B (1973) *Utilitarianism: For and Against*, Cambridge University Press, Cambridge.

Taylor, H (2018) *Social Justice in Contemporary Housing: Applying Rawls Difference Principle*, Routledge, London.

Warburton, N (2014) *Philosophy: The Classics* (4th Edition), Routledge, Abingdon.

Watts, B & Fitzpatrick, S (2018) *Welfare Conditionality*, Routledge, Abingdon.

Wolff, R (1991) *Robert Nozick: Property, Justice and the Minimal State*, Polity, Cambridge.

Žižek, S (2000) *The Fragile Absolute: Or Why is the Christian Legacy Worth Fighting For?*, Verso, London.

4   Supported housing – past and present

This chapter looks at care and supported housing in its historical context using path dependency as a framework. The various policy initiatives are placed within their historical and philosophical contexts and the reasons for the success or failure of these policies discussed. There have been several ways that the government has attempted to alleviate poverty and provide services for people who require support, supported housing or care.

The nature of social policy has changed to reflect complexity of society and has indeed been influenced by these wider changes. As capitalism succeeded feudalism, so has social policy developed to manage this change and the urbanisation of society; providing a workforce that is adequately healthy and literate (Dean, 2008). Early policies to address poverty often operated via the criminal law, for example, the *Vagrancy Act 1547* allowed the enslavement of vagabonds for two years and the beating and chaining of these slaves as well as feeding of only bread and water.

This chapter divides policy initiatives in this area divided into four periods, the Poor Law to the Industrial Revolution, the Industrial Revolution to the World Wars, the post-war consensus and Thatcherism to the present.

The Poor Law – old and new to the Industrial Revolution

Main implementation style – top-down
Philosophical underpinning – liberal/paternalism

The "Poor Law" was the earliest attempt to provide support to the poor and vulnerable. It was not one piece of legislation but rather a collection of national and local laws that made provision for those considered vulnerable. Whilst it was far from the universal safety net that we think of today, the significance of these laws is that they represent an attempt to deal with poverty via a system of support rather than criminalisation; removing responsibility from those charged with enforcing the criminal law and onto the early "welfare state".

The *Act for the Relief of the Poor 1597* established a relatively simple (top-down) implementation framework by appointing "Overseers of the Poor", individuals who were responsible for distributing money, food and other essentials to those in poverty. This Act was amended in 1601 to enable the creation of almshouses or poorhouses for those unable to care for themselves, as the Act termed them, the impotent poor. Almshouses had been around for some years running parallel to other measures to assist the poor. These were originally linked to monasteries and charitable donations from merchants, landowners and other people of means. (see Pannell and Thomas [1999] for a further history of almshouses).

However, assistance from the state came at a price. The able-bodied poor were set to work in a "House of Industry" where materials were provided for the poor to work productively, the idle poor (presumably those who refused to work in a House of Industry) were sent to a House of Correction or even prison whilst pauper children would become apprentices. Implicit in these changes is the clear recognition first that the state has a role to play in alleviating poverty and second that accommodation is a key part of supporting the poor and vulnerable. The system drew no distinction between the elderly, those with learning disabilities or other paupers, those who did not have the resources to house, clothe and feed themselves all fell under the remit of the same Poor Law measures.

The Old Poor Law is important in that it was the first time that policymakers had tackled poverty in a structured manner and through the organs of the state and brought previously voluntary services into the ambit of social policy. It also introduced the idea that state assistance is not free, and some recompense is required in the form of work. Rather than a "big bang" (as is sometimes thought), the Old Poor Law was a period of incremental change based in both national and local legislation. The state at this time was minimal and administered under a feudal system, implementation of the Poor Law would have been through a relatively simple system of "overseers" and basic state provision of Houses of Industry (where paupers worked in return for accommodation/money) or Houses of Correction (where those who refused to work in Houses of Industry were "corrected"). These institutions were run by local officers of the state appointed by individual parishes.

The creation of a state-funded structure of assistance is the beginning of a new policy paradigm and instruments (Hall, 1993). The policy paradigm had clearly shifted from one of providing for oneself and one's family to one of the State conceding that it has role in supporting those who are unable to support themselves, although a focus on the family being the prime caring unit remained. This basic paradigm has not changed much since; the state has never ceased to accept responsibility for the vulnerable, as questionable as its methods may have sometimes been. The policy instruments the Poor Law introduced were basic and moved the system from family support to one of support from the local parish. The next development would move the policy paradigm and instruments to national level.

The *Poor Law Amendment Act (PLAA) 1834* implemented the recommendations of the *Royal Commission into the Operation of the Poor Law 1832* bringing provision under a single system of administration (rather than the parish-based system that had been in place). A Poor Law Commission was established to oversee the operation of the new system at national level. Parishes were now clustered into Poor Law Unions (each run by a Poor Law Board) and union workhouses established to provide relief to the poor in the area covered by each union. Relief to the poor was provided both as "outside relief" or financial or charitable relief provided directly to the poor or as "inside relief", the workhouse. As the name suggests, the workhouse (a development of the House of Industry) was a place where the poor were provided with unpaid work, which paid for their board and lodgings.

During the 1840s, the workhouse became the only avenue of relief to the poor; other forms of relief being discouraged rather than abolished. However, as before, the workhouses did not distinguish between the circumstances of paupers. It was often thought that workhouses also acted as a deterrent to poverty through their reputation of brutality but as Crowther (1981) notes, the reality was often more one of neglect and boredom.

What is notable about these measures is the establishment of a formal (top-down) implementation structure of institutional services providing accommodation and support to the poor and needy (Irving-Clarke, 2016). Services were now overseen and administered from the centre of government rather than from individual parishes. Bringing the Poor Law system under a national framework underlined policymakers' determination to deal with the issue and enshrined supporting vulnerable people as a subject to be taken seriously by government. This was also the beginning of care and support provision to build their own policies and institutions (Kay, 2005). If these are the building blocks of path dependency, care and support now had a national basis for service provision and acceptance from national government that this was an area that merited such attention. The provision of government-employed staff and investment in buildings to house the poor and needy is surely a sign of building a path that would be difficult to reverse. If these changes to the paradigm and instruments were changing the face of care and support policy, one of the most significant paradigm shifts in history was about to begin, the Industrial Revolution. This was to affect society profoundly and mean significant change for the care and support landscape. The role of government in many policy areas expanded rapidly and it is against this backdrop that services for vulnerable people developed.

The Industrial Revolution to World War 2

Main implementation style – top-down
Philosophical underpinning – liberal/paternalism

Until the Industrial Revolution, there was little distinction between paupers, the elderly, physically disabled and mentally ill who were treated in the same manner in terms of their poverty (Means et al., 2008). Some "vulnerable" people had been able to work to support themselves but the increase in the use of technology and other social changes caused by the new industries such as new working hours and the breakdown of local/rural communities largely dispensed with the labour of elderly males (MacNicol, 2006). People with physical disabilities were excluded from the workplace by machinery designed to be operated by the able-bodied thus increasing their reliance upon welfare services; many ended up living in Poor Law institutions (Drake, 2001). Likewise, adults unable to work because of learning disabilities faced a stark choice; either live in the family home with little to no support from statutory services or live in an institution or *"mental handicap hospital"* (Fyson et al., 2007, p. 1). The Poor Law system of providing for paupers in workhouses, perhaps brutal, neglectful or both continued until 1929.

The *Local Government Act 1929* made significant changes to the structures for providing support. The best Poor Law hospitals were now retitled "Public Health Hospitals" and removed from the Poor Law system to the remit of local health authority committees. These concentrated on those with acute conditions; the elderly were viewed as chronic cases and so stayed in the remit of the workhouses (Baggott, 2004). The remaining hospital provision and workhouses were moved to the jurisdiction of counties and county boroughs, required to establish a "Public Assistance Committee" (PAC) with workhouses retitled "Public Assistance Institutions" (PAI).

Despite the existence of a growing structure to care and support vulnerable and sick people, the subsequent *Poor Law Act 1930* (note the retention of "Poor Law") kept the focus of providing for the vulnerable, including the elderly, squarely with the family.

> It should be the duty of the father, grandfather, mother, grandmother, husband or child of a poor, old, blind, lame or impotent person or other poor person not able to work, if possessed of sufficient means, to relieve and maintain that person not able to work.
>
> Quoted in Means et al. (2008, p. 23)

These developments saw the development of a nascent National Health Service (NHS) with the establishment of Public Health Hospitals (under local health authorities) whilst the workhouse system remained to support chronic cases. For the first time this produces a two-tier system of care and support, dividing acute and chronic cases and separate administrative structures for each, adding complexity. It is also an early example of the chronically sick (including the elderly) being a low-priority group for services.

The biggest change at this time was in the treatment of people with learning disabilities and/or mental health problems. Such people or "lunatics" as they were then termed, were seen as a source of major disruption in the union workhouses (Murphy, 1991). Unruly and unpredictable behaviour was not only a *"burden to both inmates and staff"* (*ibid*, p. 34) but they were also unable to work. This led to workhouse guardians adding their voice to others for these individuals to be removed elsewhere. The numbers of people detained in "lunatic asylums" ballooned at this time, they effectively became dumping grounds for people whose families could not or would not care for them or for those who either refused to or were unable to labour in the workhouses or to earn their own living independently (Murphy, 1991). The policy goal was to get the disruptive and unproductive out of the workhouses.

As a result of campaigning by reformers seized of the need for a therapeutic environment for "lunatics" supported by forward-thinking physicians, the *Lunacy Act 1845* required the building of "lunatic asylums" in all counties and created the Lunacy Commission to regulate asylums and hospitals (private, voluntary and public) where lunatics were likely to be treated. Unlike in other areas, authorities grasped the nettle and began to build large asylums that, as Murphy (1991) notes, were often architecturally, externally impressive monuments of civic pride (in contrast with their drab interiors and reputation). Murphy (*ibid*) argues that the asylum system was designed to be a therapeutic environment where a gentle regime of rewards and punishments could be used to treat patients. She does this also accepting that this was not the reality. Scull (1993) takes a rather more cynical view, seeing asylums as places where families could offload those whom they considered a burden. Gibbons (1988) argues that there were growing numbers of people, detained in ever larger institutions with fewer therapeutic pretensions. By 1890 there were 86,067 certified cases of insanity in England and Wales, a fourfold increase over the previous 45 years.

The *Royal Commission on Care and Control of the Feeble Minded 1908* and subsequent *Mental Deficiency Act 1913* defined people with learning disabilities as idiots, imbeciles or the feeble-minded depending upon the level of their learning disability; it also created a new group, the *"moral imbecile"* for people whose learning disability made them prone to *"loose morals"*. There was a second major expansion of people compulsorily detained in institutions. Figures from Tredgold (1952) quoted by Malin et al. (1980) indicate a rise from 12,000 in 1920 to 90,000 by 1939. Numbers detained eventually peaked in 1954 at over 148,000.

Most asylums detained people in large isolated colonies (Means et al., 2008), Scull (1993) coined the term *"warehouses of the unwanted"* to describe what he saw as the detention of people who society was keen to be rid of. The regime of such institutions was summarised by the *Report of the Mental Deficiency Committee 1929* (quoted in Means et al., 2008, p. 36). It was damning to say the least. However, Gladstone (1996) found that the Victorian period was often a time of optimism with regard to the training and education of people with learning disabilities even if this often meant their incarceration under the *Idiots Act 1886*.

More positively, the *Mental Health Treatment Act 1930* changed the name of "asylums" to "Mental Health Hospitals" and also introduced new categories of voluntary and temporary patients. The act established a single, unified service that took people with mental illness away from all other mainstream services (Ryan & Thomas, 1980). Pearce (2007) argues that this led to more people coming forward at an earlier stage of their mental health problems and also led to the introduction of more innovative treatments. However, he balances this by pointing out it also led to the rapid expansion of *"…unpleasant and hazardous shock therapies"* (p. 128). Once an individual had been detained, it was in the power of the Board of Control to block the release of anyone they considered unfit to live in the community, although there were safeguards. But as Means et al. (2008) point out, it was all too easy to secure the admission of any person with a learning disability. It also left other groups such as the homeless vulnerable to "certification" regardless of their mental abilities.

In 1941, the situation of a system under severe stress had led the Minister of Health to appoint ten survey teams to gather information about existing hospital services with a view to planning for the future. This produced what became known as the *"Domesday Book of Hospital Services"* (Means et al., 2008, p. 25). This represented a departure from past approaches in that it showed an attempt to get a full picture of the situation with reference to care and support for vulnerable groups.

The report showed a system that institutionalised people in need of care by banding them all together in large hospitals with the sharpest criticism reserved for the treatment of the chronic sick including the elderly. The system was criticised for not providing early treatments that could enable some to return to their homes and went on to recommend that all such patients be fully assessed and treated with a view to returning them to *"maximum activity"* (Nuffield Provincial Hospital Trust, 1946, p. 16). Those for whom treatment was considered unsuccessful or ineffective would be retained in hospital but even then, their condition should have been kept under regular review. The report blamed this situation and the haphazard growth in health services on the lack of strategic planning and raised awareness of the cost of these blocked beds.

During this period there was a theme of good intentions being followed through by poor implementation of policy objectives. Services were swamped by large numbers of service users, possibly dumped by families incapable of or unwilling to care for them. The chronically ill (including the elderly) were treated as a low-priority group and shut away from society, denying them a political voice. Good intentions were also undermined by the emerging science of genetics which held that intelligence is innate and raised alarm over the high birth rate amongst the poorest groups in society. The idea that this could lead to a contamination of the genetic stock of the country led to the removal of "defectives" from society and their placement in generic asylums to prevent them reproducing (Means et al., 2008).

The outbreak of World War 2 produced another key period in the history of care and support. The creation of a 300,000 bed emergency medical service resulted in the discharge of 140,000 hospital patients in two days (Morris, 1969); inevitably many of these will have been elderly patients, another example of the low status of the elderly and services providing for their care. The next section looks at World War 2 and the post-war consensus that followed and how this affected vulnerable groups.

The post-war consensus to Thatcher

Main implementation style – top-down/bureaucracy
Philosophical style – social democracy (1st way)/Paternalism

World War 2 provided another key period in the "path" of provision care and support that continue to shape provision to the present day. Suggestions that there should be a unified system to provide healthcare pre-dated the hostilities of World War 2 by some years (Baggott, 2004). Indeed, some members of the 1909 Royal Commission on the Poor Laws had produced a minority report (Cd 4499, 1909) promoting the principle of free healthcare for the poor as a right. The minority report proved too radical at the time, but during World War 2 the idea of comprehensive healthcare became "… *bound up with the broader aim of reconstructing Britain*" (Baggott, 2004, p. 84). Although there were questions about the scope and nature of this service, the Beveridge Report (Cmd 6404, 1942) set out the broad framework for the post-war welfare state. The subsequent creation of the NHS in 1946 brought all hospital accommodation including PAIs under the same administrative structure. In addition, Doctors remembered the shell-shocked and battle-damaged soldiers of the World War 1 and resolved that this would not be repeated.

This led to services for people with learning disabilities and mental health problems becoming more mainstream; asylums were renamed hospitals, becoming the responsibility of regional hospital boards. The *National Health Service Act 1946* made local authorities responsible for the initial care and removal to hospital of persons dealt with under the Lunacy and Mental Treatment Acts; the ascertainment and (where necessary) removal to institutions of mental defectives and supervision, guardianship, training and occupation of those in the community under Mental Deficiency Acts; and prevention, care and after-care of all types of patients, so far as this was not otherwise provided for. The first two are statutory duties whilst the third only a permissive power which authorities proved reluctant to use (Means et al., 2008), thus wasting the opportunity for community-based treatment.

Services for the mentally ill remained of low status, for example, Goodwin (1990) notes that during the early 1950s, mental deficiency hospitals had 40% of all patients but only 20% of funding. He also notes large discrepancies between the proportional increases in funding for mental health services and other service areas, this he uses to support the tag of "Cinderella Services" for mental health services.

Despite this there was considerable optimism for the treatment of mental illness and early treatment for soldiers traumatised at the front-line paid dividends and led to an explosion in experimental treatments. The treatment of soldiers during and after World War 2 had led to experimental new treatments such as Electro-Convulsive Therapy (ECT) and Insulin Coma Therapy (ICT). Despite the misplaced belief in the efficacy of such treatments, they raised hopes that those with serious mental health problems could be treated and return to live in the community (Murphy, 1991). Alongside these treatments the introduction of anti-psychotic drugs had a huge impact on the treatment of people with mental disorders (*ibid*).

However, the changes did little to stop poor treatment of older patients with numerous reports highlighting the shortcomings in care for the elderly (Samson, 1944, Nuffield Provincial Hospitals Trust 1946, Rowntree Report, 1980). Large institutions housed as many as 1,500 people with numerous diagnoses; these institutions were often poorly maintained and ran restrictive regimes (not so different from the workhouse). There were also voices from the medical establishment calling for a geriatric speciality to drive up the standard of care for the elderly. However, this remained a low-status route for medical professionals and a low priority for funding (Martin, 1995).

The *National Assistance Act 1948* had the potential to provide another key "path dependency" moment in terms of care and support services, by giving local authorities the power to "...*promote the welfare of those who are blind, deaf, dumb and others who are substantially and permanently handicapped by illness, injury or congenital deformity*" (s.29). This was a reaction to the great number of people returning from World War 2 with physical and mental impairments and the resultant pressure upon the newly founded NHS. The potential would not be realised.

It remained beyond the power of local authorities to set up preventative services for the elderly with the exception of home care where authority was provided by the *NHS Act 1946*. Local authorities could not set up meals on wheels, chiropody, laundry schemes, befriending or counselling services, etc. that would have eased the lot of elderly people in need (Means et al., 2008). Parker (1965) commented that

> The concern to maintain and foster family life evident in the Children Act was completely lacking in the National Assistance Act. The latter made no attempt to provide any sort of substitute family life for old people who could no longer be supported by their own relatives. Institutional provision was accepted without question.
>
> (p. 106)

Eyden (1965) was also damning in her critique of the implementation of the Act.

> It is clear…that if local authorities implement to the full this legislation in close cooperation with voluntary organisations, all groups of the handicapped or their families should have a comprehensive service to which they can turn to meet any of their specialised needs. Unfortunately, this has not been the case. The duty of providing services was continued under the National Assistance Act only for the blind. The Ministry of Health in Circular 32/51 issued guidance to local authorities on the provision of welfare services to other classes of handicapped persons in August 1951, and local authorities were invited to submit schemes and their subsequent implementation was not made compulsory until 1960. As a result, the development of services for the deaf and other categories of handicapped persons over the past sixteen years has been patchy and inadequate.
>
> (p. 171)

This confirmed the reality that older people were a low-status group in terms of the assistance offered by the state; far from the only occasion where crises in other policy areas took priority. Instead, the thrust of thinking at the time was that domiciliary services were an extra that could be provided by voluntary sector organisations and charities such as the Women's Royal Voluntary Service (WRVS, now the Royal Voluntary Service, RVS) and

Red Cross. The end result of this was that services for elderly people developed in a piecemeal way (much as supported housing services later did) confirming criticisms of poor planning in the past and attempts to develop the planning role of local authorities (Nuffield Provincial Hospital Trust 1946; Sumner & Smith, 1969).

What followed (in an echo of the old Poor Law) was a number of pieces of legislation that gradually added to the powers of local authorities to provide services for elderly people despite the growing research evidence of the lack of services being provided by the voluntary sector (Means et al., 2008). For example, the *National Assistance (Amendment) Act 1962* allowed local authorities to provide meal services for the first time (thus far they had only had the power to provide grants to the voluntary sector to provide this). The *Health Services and Public Health Act 1968* gave local authorities the general power to promote the health and well-being of elderly people. Implementation of the 1968 Act was delayed until 1971 to allow the set-up of unified social services departments within local authorities. Also, the *National Health Service Act 1977* made the provision of home care a mandatory duty instead of a discretionary power as it had been thus far.

The *Mental Health Act 1959* (the result of a three-year Royal Commission on mental illness and mental deficiency between 1954 and 1957) restructured services for people with mental health issues removing the legislative framework for the constraint of such people and instead envisaging a system of local authority which provided services such as day care, hostels, social work support and sheltered employment schemes. Murphy (1991) notes that this was a time of significant steps forward. The act backed voluntary treatment and safeguards on detention were introduced and the UK became something of an example of forward-thinking treatments. Enoch Powell, despite his dubious views on other policy areas, was a powerful advocate for the humane treatment of people with mental health problems (Murphy, 1991). Drawing on his experiences visiting large hospitals and being impressed with attempts to set up community-based treatments by some superintendents, Powell resolved to close the majority of mental hospitals as they stood at the time.

The 1962 Hospital Plan set out the closure programme in full and the first comprehensive surveys of health and welfare plans found a "...*thriving, buoyant and committed local government eager to rise to the challenge*" (Murphy, 1991, p. 59). However, Murphy is damning about the failure to deliver, dubbing the years 1962–1990 the "Disaster Years" (p. 60).

Policy at this time had a dual-pronged approach to delivering services for people with mental health issues and/or learning disabilities. The first, and more prominent, was the provision of inpatient and outpatient treatment and services by district general hospitals provided and funded via the

NHS. The second, and much lower key, was the provision of a network of hostels, "home" accommodation, social work support, day care and sheltered work for the chronically mentally disabled to provide an alternative to the wards of hospitals. Murphy (1991) likens the former to a *"major symphonic work"* whilst the latter as *"barely audible until the 80s"* (p. 60).

To illustrate her point, she asserts that by 1974 there were 60,000 fewer residents in large "mental hospitals", but few community services to take up their treatment. However, of this 60,000 Murphy (1991) states that many were socially competent or cured and able to look after themselves, at least in the short term; others returned to the care of their families. Many beds were also closed as their occupants died and therefore disappeared from the official statistics. It is very difficult to know the true picture as no follow-up work was done and few records were kept (Murphy, 1991). On a positive note, enthusiastic psychiatrists, who did follow up cases either via outpatients' departments or a growing Community Psychiatric Nurse (CPN) service, drove early discharges (*ibid*).

From the information available to her, Murphy (1991) asserts that we do know that many of those discharged suffered relapses or the discharge arrangements broke down. Many of these people ended up in boarding houses, bed and breakfast accommodation or even prison. She notes that there may have been some successes, but we have no records and therefore no way of knowing. By 1974 it was evident that the community services envisaged had not materialised. The Department of Health and Social Security (DHSS) white paper *Better Services for the Mentally Ill* (DHSS, 1975) admitted that such services were unlikely to be in decent shape for another 25 years. The oil crisis and public-spending constraint during the 1970s meant that hopes for the expansion of domiciliary care services were dashed. Instead the debate shifted away from talk of expansion to the rebalancing of residential and domiciliary care services (Means et al., 2002).

Services for older people were beleaguered by research evidence that social services departments prioritised services hierarchically with elderly people at the bottom (a familiar theme); provision of such services was considered to be mundane and routine as such allocated to untrained staff (Bowl, 1986). In addition, the death of Maria Colwell in 1973 ensured the focus of social services departments was centred squarely on child protection at the expense of other service areas (Parton, 1991).

It was not all doom and gloom however; Murphy (1991) found that some innovative, quality services, for the mentally ill, had sprung up although he does qualify this by stating that these were *"fragmented, un-coordinated, haphazard and extraordinarily variable from place to place"* (p. 63). In addition, Murphy (1991) paints a picture of overburdened families struggling to cope, people with mental health problems sleeping rough, patients discharged from psychiatric wards to bed and breakfast accommodation and short-term hospital beds blocked by the homeless with no help in terms of rehabilitation or sheltered accommodation to assist them.

Although the government took steps to promote community care via two white papers during the 1970s, "Better Services for the Mentally Handicapped" (1971) and "Better Services for the Mentally Ill" (1975), take-up by local authorities remained low. The Audit Commission report entitled "Making a Reality of Community Care" (1986) found only limited action on improving hospital provision and no movement at all on developing community services. In short, both groups remained a low priority for both local and national government. It is difficult to be sure about the standard of services in the 40 years between 1946 and 1986; such was the lack of good record-keeping or even interest from government (Means et al., 2008; Murphy, 1991). Means et al. quote an excerpt from the diaries of Frank Thomas of life inside a large mental hospital portraying a picture of institutional neglect remarkably similar to earlier accounts (Samson, 1944 referenced in Means et al., 2008, p. 26). This excerpt paints a picture of an austere physical and social environment with nothing to keep patients occupied or stimulated, of vulnerable people utterly neglected.

Miller and Gwynn (1972) produced a comprehensive study of residential provision in the post-war period that revealed many of the inadequacies of the system. These were similar to those in the care of the elderly highlighted by Townsend (1964), i.e. failure to implement community services. Miller and Gwynn (1972) make the further observation that disabled people were often offered care placements that lasted their whole adult lives. This, they say, rendered many effectively *"socially dead"* society having *"washed its hands of them"* (p. 89).

By 1984 the number of hospital beds for people with mental health problems reduced by a further 25,000, a total of 69,000 beds closed. At the same time, there were only 3,500 local authority residential and day-care places available, some 48,000 short of the recommended number needed. These shortfalls also affected new patients. Murphy (1991) laments a lack of therapeutic beds in hospitals and points to a lack of choice about treatments and general dissatisfaction with services as signs of acute policy and service failure. Many were left in emergency, temporary accommodation (often bed and breakfast) paid for by the local authority; it was clear that community care was failing vulnerable people. Added to this, Murphy (1991) notes an increasing number of very elderly people putting further pressure on services.

Use of controversial therapies such as ECT and some forms of medication raised issues regarding the rights of patients (and rightly so), numerous stories in the popular press-exposed cases of physical and mental cruelty within institutions. In addition, academic studies such as Robb (1967) and Morris (1969) discovered poor conditions and poor treatment in hospitals. This was balanced however by studies such as Jones (1972) that bemoaned the exaggeration of such cases by the press who often sought to portray them as the norm rather than the exception. There was a lack of community services for both children and adults with learning disabilities, a few residential homes or hostels had appeared and some local authorities had developed training facilities in the community and appointed Mental Welfare Officers to make routine visits to family homes to give support (Atkinson, 1988).

During the 1970s, Alf Morris MP tabled a private members bill to try to force local authorities to provide comprehensive services for the sick and disabled. This bill became the *Chronically Sick and Disabled Persons Act 1970*. This imposed duties upon local authorities to provide services rather than merely the power to do so but was not supported by the additional resources necessary to implement them. This meant that the disabled had to compete with all other groups for local authority funding (Topliss, 1979).

On a positive note, the act acknowledged that younger disabled people were a distinct category from elderly people and should have separate care solutions. However, the story, once again, is one of local authorities failing to implement the apparent intentions of the policymakers. Most local authorities continued to place younger physically disabled people in homes for the elderly. A minority of local authorities set up specialist homes for the physically disabled, but this was very much the exception rather than the norm. This neglect continued in the face of evidence that the number of disabled people had increased due to the effects of World War 2, the polio epidemic and longer life expectancies due to medical advances. Means et al. (2008) note that statistics on the number of younger disabled people in elderly care homes are hard to come by although they do note Leat (1998) and Harrison (1986) as having produced studies showing that provision for disabled people was minimal to say the least.

By the 1970s, there was widespread agreement from all sides of the political spectrum that the hierarchical and monolithic bureaucracies that dominated local authorities needed radical reform. The monolithic welfare state had served a purpose but badly needed modernisation (Foord & Simic, 2005). This was a result of several factors. Firstly, there were a number of scandals related to the large-scale institutions that provided services for vulnerable people. Public disquiet regarding these institutions had existed since the 19th century but studies by Barton (1959), Goffman (1961, 1970) and Robb (1967) set out in some detail the failures of the system. Particularly striking was Goffman's concept of the "*total institution*", places completely cut off from the outside world.

This was coupled with a period of economic pressure during the 1970s where high public spending was seen as part of the problem to be solved (Malpass & Murie, 1999). Malpass and Murie argue that spending restraint was already locked in by 1979, but the election of the Conservative Party under the leadership of Margaret Thatcher was to have a dramatic and resounding impact on supported housing services. This is explored in the next section.

Thatcherism and new public management

Main implementation style – hybrid top-down/bottom-up/policy networks
Philosophical underpinning – "Thatcherism" (2nd way)/New Public Management

The story of modern supported housing began with the election of Margaret Thatcher in 1979. The changes wrought by her governments (and of John Major) have had long-lasting effects. Thatcher was building upon systems that had failed. Following the significant history of neglect, pressure for reform again built up during the late 1980s. The Conservative government asked Sir Roy Griffiths to produce a report reviewing the funding and organisation of community care.

"Community Care: An Agenda for Action" or Griffiths Report (DHSS, 1988), proposed a radical strategy to reform the provision of community care. The report proposed a greater role for the private and voluntary sectors in providing care to vulnerable people and also the creation of a quasi-market for care provision (residential and domiciliary). The report fed into the white paper *"Caring for People"* (HMSO, 1989) and the subsequent *National Health Service and Community Care Act 1990*. The white paper and act followed the recommendations of the Griffiths Report almost to the letter. However, there were two notable recommendations that were not implemented.

First, the Griffiths Report had recommended that a "Minister for Community Care" be appointed to lead the reforms and second a new system of "ear-marked funds" for community care services. It would be easy to see this lack of leadership and funding as a sign that the government was less than fully committed to reforms.

The government was distrustful of local authority's spending ambitions and particularly disliked the proposal to give local authorities a key role (Baggott, 2004), although there was a limited sum of ring-fenced funding for services for people with severe mental health problems and also drug and alcohol dependency. The main funding stream would be via the revenue support grant system. The lack of ring-fenced funds for community care remains controversial (Means et al., 2008).

The act did, however, contain major reform. The strategic thrust of the act was twofold, first to put in place a system of "care management" and second to create a mixed market of care. In order to accomplish this, the act gave social services departments a lead strategic role as the "arrangers and purchasers" of care. The main responsibilities were threefold.

- Carry out an appropriate assessment of an individuals need for so-cial care (including residential and nursing home care), including collaboration as necessary with medical, nursing and other caring agencies before deciding what services should be provided. (Care Management)
- Design packages of services tailored to meet the assessed needs of individuals and their carers and the appointment of a 'Case Man-ager' to facilitate this. (Care Management)
- Secure the delivery of services, not simply by acting as direct pro-viders, but by developing their purchasing and contracting role to become 'enabling authorities'. (Creating a mixed market of care)

DoH (1989, p. 17) quoted in
Means et al. (2008, pp. 53/54)

Enabling authorities would have the power to commission and purchase services from the statutory, voluntary and private sectors and shape ser-vices to meet the needs of those who needed them; needs-led rather than service-led.

Means et al. (2008) outline the success of the reforms. The underlying aim of limiting expenditure on independent sector provision had been achieved and a *"needs led, yet cash limited system"* (p. 82) introduced. Local authorities had been successful in limiting their role as direct providers and transformed themselves into purchasers and commissioners; the result of this was the expansion of the independent sector in providing day and domiciliary care and services. Frail older people could now access services that supported them in their own home rather than rely on residential care; younger disabled people are able to access a wide range of services via direct payments, exercising greater control over the organisation and de-livery of support. Although policy networks had been part of the landscape for some years (Rhodes, 1997), the introduction of providers external to the state was the beginning of a widened "policy network", thus diffusing power and responsibility to a wider array of organisations and individuals – including those to whom the state had no direct line of accountability to.

However, there were also significant problems with the new system, a return to some familiar themes. Funding, or the lack of it, was the main complaint from local authorities and independent providers alike. Once again, chronic underfunding for "community care" made it impossible to provide quality services and threatened some independent organisations with closure. Social services departments routinely spent more on care than was allocated in funding settlements from central government and that this had a knock-on effect on the development of services and funding of other services for which they were responsible (Means et al., 2008). By way of illustration, local authorities were spending 8.9% more than allocated to care provision by 2000–2001 (*ibid*).

The decision to allocate funding via the general local authority revenue grant system rather than as a ring-fenced sum (as proposed by the Griffiths Report), allowed local authorities to channel funding into other service areas that were considered a higher priority. The role of care managers as gatekeepers to services for local authorities meant that their role became as much about rationing access to services and therefore limiting expenditure as anything else. This made it difficult for them to also promote individual choice and self-determination (Rummery, 2002).

There was also criticism that in response to the challenge of introducing the new regime and inadequate funding, local authorities responded with unnecessary levels of bureaucracy; concentrating on implementing structures and processes from the outset the experiences of practitioners and service users were given much less attention (Lewis & Glennerster, 1996). There was evidence that the commissioning process was both costly and bureaucratic, exacerbated by poor relationships between commissioners and providers (Baggott, 2004). Those trying to access services were often confused by the systems and procedures they encountered and the information they received (Rummery & Glendinning, 1999).

On another familiar theme, there were issues surrounding the recruitment, training and retention of staff confirming the low-grade status of front-line care workers; many of who received close to the minimum wage for what was a challenging and demanding job (Hadley & Clough, 1996). There was also a tendency to try and fit existing services to needs, rather than remodelling services to fit need (Hawley & Hudson, 1996).

Since the 1989 white paper (HMSO, 1989), there has been radical change in the way services are provided. Greater use of community care and the expanding independent sector have both been delivered with some success, however, inadequate funding bedevilled the system. Services were designed to suit the bureaucratic processes of local authorities (see Seddon, 2008), and were not responsive to the needs of service users; staff were not valued adequately in relation to the role that they carried out.

The care and support sector continued to develop throughout the 1980s partly due to the campaign for supported living for people with learning disabilities and disability rights movement. Supported living became recognised as one of the most important ways people can be empowered and supported (Fyson et al., 2007) and based upon a number of values that recognise the rights and responsibilities of the individual in exercising choice about the way that they live (*ibid*).

The role of housing policy

Housing (as a specific policy area) has a surprisingly short history in the area of providing care and support. As discussed earlier, prior to World War 2, there was little distinction between paupers; accommodation for the poor and vulnerable was provided via Houses of Industry or Correction, the workhouse or asylums. Housing policy as we know it today only began with the modern welfare state (in 1945) with the mass construction of council housing (now known as social housing). Housing policy as a specific subset for providing support has an even shorter history. The policy history of duties to homeless people is relevant here as it prescribes those groups who are considered to be in need or vulnerable and has therefore had a profound effect on the groups living in supported accommodation.

Prior to the *National Assistance Act 1948*, provision for homeless people consisted of large, poor-quality converted workhouses and resettlement units, known as "spikes" with shared dormitories, they were predominantly associated with single, white, middle-aged "men of the road" with alcohol problems (Neale, 1997). Hostel provision continued to be large and basic, some having up to 100 beds. This accommodation was primarily used for emergencies and for those excluded from accessing other accommodation, legitimised because people were in desperate need of physical shelter and would otherwise have slept rough (Busch-Geertsema & Sahlin, 2007).

The first duty to house homeless people was placed upon local authorities by the *Housing (Homelessness Persons) Act 1977*. Those with a "priority need", "unintentionally homeless" and with a "local connection" qualified for statutory rights and were, by law, provided with temporary hostel provision, whilst settled accommodation was sought (Jones & Pleace, 2010). Section 29(1) of the Act gave local authorities a duty to promote the welfare of those

> persons aged 18 or over, who are blind, or dumb, or suffer from mental disorder of any description and other persons aged 18 or over who are substantially & permanently handicapped by illness, injury or congenital deformity or other such disabilities as may be prescribed by the minister.

This was one of the early attempts to define a specific group as "vulnerable" and therefore entitled to specific state services. The *Housing Act 1996* made new requirements on local authorities to make provision for groups of homeless individuals and families defined as such in Part 7. The 1996 Act defined five groups who must be accepted as in priority need, these are

- pregnant women, or any person who resides with a pregnant woman
- households with whom dependent children reside or might reasonably be expected to reside
- all 16- and 17-year-olds, provided they are not a "relevant child" (relevant children remain the responsibility of social services) or a child in need to whom a local authority owes a duty under Section 20 of the Children Act 1989
- all 18- to 20-year-olds (other than "relevant students"), who "at any time after reaching the age of sixteen, but while still under eighteen" were, but are no longer, looked after, accommodated or fostered
- any person who has lost her/his accommodation as a result of an emergency such as flood, fire or other disaster.

It also defined the following groups who must be accepted as in priority need provided that the authority is satisfied that they are vulnerable as a result of

- old age, mental illness or disability, physical disability or other special reason, or someone who lives with one of these categories of vulnerable person
- having been looked after, accommodated or fostered and is aged 21 or over (other than "relevant students")
- having been a member of Her Majesty's regular naval, military or air forces
- having served a custodial sentence, been committed for contempt of court or similar offence, or been remanded in custody
- having had to leave accommodation because of violence or threats of violence from another person that are likely to be carried out.

The definition underwent another overhaul with the *Homelessness Act 2002*. Priority need now encompassed

- a pregnant woman or a person with whom she resides or might reasonably be expected to reside
- a person with whom dependent children reside or might reasonably be expected to reside
- a person who is vulnerable as a result of old age, mental illness or handicap or physical disability or other special reason, or with whom such a person resides or might reasonably be expected to reside

- a person aged 16 or 17 who is not a "relevant child" or a child in need to whom a local authority owes a duty under Section 20 of the Children Act 1989
- a person under 21 who was (but is no longer) looked after, accommodated or fostered between the ages of 16 and 18 (except a person who is a "relevant student")
- a person aged 21 or more who is vulnerable as a result of having been looked after, accommodated or fostered (except a person who is a "relevant student")
- a person who is vulnerable as a result of having been a member of Her Majesty's regular naval, military or air forces
- a person who is vulnerable as a result of

  a   having served a custodial sentence,
  b   having been committed for contempt of court or any other kindred offence, or
  c   having been remanded in custody

- a person who is vulnerable as a result of ceasing to occupy accommodation because of violence from another person or threats of violence from another person which are likely to be carried out
- a person who is vulnerable for any other special reason, or with whom such a person resides or might reasonably be expected to reside
- a person who is homeless, or threatened with homelessness, as a result of an emergency such as flood, fire or other disaster.

This definition persists in England to the present day. It is significant as it represents the point at which responsibility for certain groups of people passed from social services departments to housing departments. Part 7 of the 1996 Act places a duty upon local authorities to secure interim accommodation for those it suspects are eligible for housing and assessed as being in one of the above groups, and thereafter permanent accommodation if this proves to be so. This measure clearly led to the establishment of many local authority accommodation-based services, e.g. hostels and supported housing that subsequently become funded and regulated by Supporting People. It also meant that there would need to be some kind of split between those assessed as needing residential care and those for whom this was not appropriate but who nevertheless found themselves defined as homeless under the terms of the 1996 Act. Inevitably, services set up to provide interim accommodation to such individuals would need to have some level of supportive function also in order to prepare service users for the transfer to permanent accommodation and prevent repeat homelessness. The effect this had in practice was to extend the type and numbers of people whom the local authority has duty to assist well beyond those named in community care legislation.

Alongside the Supporting People programme, the white paper "Valuing People" (DoH, 2001) set forward the New Labour government's plans for promoting rights, choice and independence for people considered vulnerable including people with learning disabilities. In this paper, the government recognised that housing and support is a crucial factor in people having more choice and control in their lives. However, despite this acknowledgement it stopped short of recommending supported living as a preferred option but instead outlined a number of options including supported living, small-scale ordinary housing and intentional communities (where people with learning disabilities live together in a created community with shared goals) (Fyson et al., 2007).

Fyson et al. (2007) also note that New Labour's Supporting People programme was a potential funding stream for implementing Valuing People objectives and that it would have provided greater flexibility for local authorities in providing services. It could also have promoted more effective joint working between health, housing and social services, long acknowledged as contributing to poor outcomes for individuals (*ibid*). It is to this that we now turn.

New Labour and the supporting people programme

Main implementation style – hybrid top-down/bottom-up
Philosophical underpinning – Third Way (Blairism?)

Launched in 2003, this was New Labour's policy programme to fund, regulate and plan support services for the vulnerable; it created a new umbrella term for these services "Housing Related Support" (HRS) (SITRA, 2014; Watson et al., 2003). The policy and practice guidance document to local authorities "Supporting People: Policy into Practice" (DETR, 2001) stated that the programme would provide HRS to people including older people, people with learning disabilities, people with mental health problems, refuge support and move-on for people fleeing domestic violence, young homeless people who may never have held a tenancy and support for people struggling with their current accommodation (p. 107).

Supporting People also brought the "third way" values of "social investment", "equality as inclusion" and "no rights without responsibility" into supported housing policy. The policy and practice guidance for local authorities (DETR, 2001) was awash not only with the language of choice, integration and partnership working but also with the language of monitoring and audit; thus, symbolising the New Labour attempt to balance the perceived gains of New Public Management (under Thatcher and Major governments) with the language and governmentalities of choice, integration and inclusion (Newman, 2001). There is also specific reference to older people and Black and Minority Ethnic (BME) people and communities in the document supporting Newman's (2001) contention that New Labour sought to explicitly include groups it perceived as excluded within the Supporting People programme.

New Labour (as with all modern governments) sought to "frame" the policy agenda and debate. Building upon the ideas of Foucault (1977, 1997) they sought to govern the "conduct of conduct" and mould governable citizens. In this vein, Newman (2014) contends that the New Labour governmentalities inclusion equality can be seen as strategies (to shape the individual and society) rather than just as outcomes. In terms of the Supporting People programme and with particular reference to homelessness and housing, the New Labour government sought to recast homelessness or rough sleeping as a situation to be avoided (much like the Victorians had before them), probably in reaction to criticism levelled at the previous Conservative governments that they had not done enough about street homelessness. Upon their election in 1997, New Labour inherited a number of problems resulting from the piecemeal approach of previous governments.

Prior to the Supporting People programme, support services had been funded via a mixture of Housing Benefit (HB) and a plethora of charitable and statutory sources (DSS, 1998). The programme dealt with the separation of funding by taking a number of funding streams (including HB) and putting them into one new stream (DSS, 1998). Because it was not clear how much HB had been used to fund support, the programme began with an initial 12-month period where providers claimed, "Transitional Housing Benefit" (THB) for each service user they worked with. Supporting People funding at this time was an uncapped, ring-fenced sum. The final amount paid or "Platinum Cut" was placed into the new fund but was considerably more than even the highest estimates (Robson Rhodes, 2004), this set the tone for the rest of the programme.

There had also been no formal structures for the strategic development of support services (DSS, 1998). Social Care services had long been driven by national, regional and local strategies but HRS services had largely been left to develop piecemeal. That is not to say that local authorities and other agencies did not carry out strategic work when commissioning/starting up new services, but that providers had led the start-up of new services by identifying a need and linking up capital and revenue funding. This led to a situation where in some areas there was over-provision of some services, e.g. generic accommodation-based supported living and undersupply of other services. Floating support was not a mainstream service type in many areas either. All Local Authority Supporting People teams were therefore required to produce a five-year strategy for service provision in their areas. This would give details of demand, existing provision and then a strategy to restructure services to more closely fit demand, as well as anticipate emerging needs and a plan to meet these (DETR, 2001).

Finally, Supported Housing providers were not inspected or audited by an external, independent body to ensure they were adhering to acceptable standards. The programme introduced both an accreditation framework to ensure the financial viability and governance strength of provider and the Quality Assessment Framework (QAF) to ensure that providers were meeting required standards of service provision and consulting their service users on provision (DETR, 2001). Accreditation and QAF inspections were carried out by the same local authority teams responsible for strategic planning.

Initially at least, the (New Labour) government showed no sign of wanting to tackle this issue but a Divisional Court judgement in 1997 held that HB could only be used to provide support such as that related to the upkeep of a building. The Audit Commission report "Home Alone" (Audit Commission, 1998) also raised many of the issues discussed above, prompting the government to review the strategic, funding and administrative structures for supported housing. The result was a consultation document (DSS, 1998) and a later policy into practice guide (DETR, 2001) outlining the new "Supporting People" programme.

Supporting People was an integrated policy that broke the link between housing and support, allowing people to receive the support they needed regardless of tenure. The system was also designed to bring together representatives from housing, health, criminal justice, social care and other services to oversee the provision of a genuinely joined up service that provided support when and where it was needed. This would be achieved by bringing representatives from each of these areas together on a commissioning body that would oversee the strategic commissioning of services and report to elected members on what should be done within the local authority area. There was also specific instruction on cross-authority working and recognition that some services crossed these boundaries and should therefore be funded as such.

The programme sub-divided services into "accommodation-based" and "non-accommodation-based" services (Baxter & Carr, 2007; DETR, 2001). DETR (2001) defined these as follows.

Accommodation-based services

This is the term commonly used in the sector to define services provided on either a temporary or permanent basis, but where accommodation is provided to the service users as part of the financial charge and contractual basis for the service. The accommodation may be in the form of a self-contained flat or a room in a cluster or block of the same type of provision (Baxter & Carr, 2007). Support is provided by staff who may have an office in the scheme or visit on a regular basis. This type of accommodation commonly includes hostels for homeless people/families, refuges for women and children at risk of domestic violence, housing for older people (often referred to as "sheltered") or foyers for young people (with provision of education and training) (there are others).

Non-accommodation-based services

Although counter-intuitive, there are services that come under the umbrella term of supported housing, where accommodation is not part of the fundamental service offer. The support provided is aimed at allowing people to maintain their tenancies, live as independently as possible and participate in civic life. This type of support expanded hugely under the Supporting People programme often described as "housing related support" (DETR, 2001; Irving-Clarke, 2016). For these reasons it is included in the definition of supported housing. Services that fall into this category include the following:

- Floating support – support provided by a visiting support worker, on a temporary basis, to allow service users to remain in their existing tenancy. (Often thought of as a "preventative service" to stop people in a crisis becoming homeless.)
- Resettlement services – these enable people who have lived in supported or temporary accommodation to transition successfully into, and sustain, a permanent home.
- Outreach services – provided (usually) to people living in an accommodation-based service but provide more specialist support, e.g. support with drug or alcohol misuse.
- Community alarm services – provided to older or vulnerable people enabling them to summon help when needed.
- Home improvement services providing aids and adaptations.

The first three have been defined as "short-term" (generally lasting for under two years) whilst the fourth is a long-term service (lasting for over two years) (see DETR, 2001).

The conditions of the programme also necessitated a more formal delineation between care and support. Funding for supported housing was placed into a single, ring-fenced funding stream; until this point it had been funded via the HB system paying support charges, service charges and rent. The result of separating support charges into a different funding stream was the necessity to put rules in place about what could and could not be funded via this new funding stream. One of the things it could not be used to pay for was personal (social) care.

There is often little practical delineation between care and support and so a system where there is a blurred line between funding streams worked quite well. Many services operated very well claiming HB for eligible parts of the services and utilising care funding to provide additional "care" when needed. Supported living for people with learning disabilities were a good example. However, the Supporting People programme demanded that these be separated, and it made clear which funding stream was funding which parts of the service. In the policy to practice document (DETR, 2001), the government proposed that (housing related) support be defined as services provided to people to enable them to be able to live independently, and that the service could one day be withdrawn. Support was put in place for this express purpose. Personal care was therefore defined as services provided to people to enable them to live as independently as possible but with the acknowledgement that they would never be able to be fully independent and would always need some level of care, often with help in carrying out personal tasks, e.g. washing or toileting.

From the inception and implementation of the programme, there was no shortage of interest in its progress. Much of the material published on Supporting People in the last decade was largely focussed upon policy and practice issues and concentrates on outcomes for service users or on specific groups (Cameron, 2009; Craigforth, 2008; Eliot & Hamilton, 2009; Fyson et al., 2007; Goldie, 2004; Holman, 2008; Scragg, 2008; Watson et al., 2003) or has been either carried out or funded by the government itself (Audit Commission 2005, 2009; CLG, 2007, 2008a, b, c, d; CLG, 2009a, 2009b; CSCI, 2006; Secretary of State, 2010).

The Audit Commission (2005, 2009), Fyson et al. (2007) and CLG Committee (2009b) highlight the successes of the programme. The Audit Commission (2005) acknowledged that the programme had allowed more independent living, could be cost-effective and contribute to desired policy outcomes across virtually all service user groups. Despite some criticisms, there were improvements in the focus on service users and carers, attention on value for money, improvements to the range and quality of services, new impetus to dealing with some long-standing issues and improved local partnership working.

It was clear that close partnerships between mainstream health, social care, housing budgets were desirable and necessary and were managed well in some areas; often associated with the better performing authorities.

Improved benchmarking had driven improvements; scrutiny of use of grant funding reduced inappropriate use and services not delivering acceptable quality were decommissioned or improved. Existing services had been remodelled reducing costs, better meeting local needs and linking services more effectively; finally, innovative approaches to service delivery had been encouraged and secured (Audit Commission, 2005).

Stronger performing authorities were characterised by ownership and integration with wider council activities, e.g. homelessness, drug and alcohol harm reduction, sustainable hospital discharge and community safety; also a shared vision between all partners, active leadership and support, review and change of staff skills and resources, an open approach that drew upon the skills of providers, service users, carers, etc. and effective review programmes that improve value for money (Audit Commission, 2005).

In these areas, Supporting People (SP) was already a mainstream service supported by other strategies and partners, but there is doubt in too many areas about whether improvements will occur. It concludes that although many of these problems can be solved locally, others are national concerns and that local gains could be lost because of uncertainty about future responsibilities, funding and lack of incentives for authorities and providers to perform well (Audit Commission, 2005).

However, the report acknowledges that the improvements noted were not evident everywhere and that there was a "significant minority" of authorities where performance was "weak" (Audit Commission 2005, p. 20; 2009, p. 27). Particularly noted was poor preparation in some authorities; some lacked adequate information on needs in their area and some had confrontational or poor relationships with providers. At worst, some authorities were making damaging cuts to service funding by making "across the board" cuts that took no account of efficiency or service quality. There was also a failure to liaise with colleagues in health or social care in order to ensure a strategic approach to service provision and "double monitoring" of services or inadequate checks (Audit Commission, 2005, p. 21).

By 2009, Supporting People had developed a strong identity underpinned by governance and a performance management framework. However, there remained some authorities where governance and performance were poor (the report doesn't say how many) (Audit Commission, [2009], p. 27). Value for money had improved with the national grant being reduced, but the number of places in SP-funded services remained broadly static whilst quality and relevance improved. There was also significant reinvestment of efficiency savings in services, meaning additional places or new high-priority services. Cap Gemini estimated a net benefit of £2.77bn from an SP investment of £1.55bn (CLG, 2009b).

Outcomes for service users had improved, greater user involvement, choice and control were noted as important factors (Audit Commission, 2009). The new outcomes framework and requirement to measure and record was also seen as important as it made providers think in a more service user centred way. There had been development of single points of access and clearer referral routes. Alongside more localised services, this had made access easier for many groups. CLG guidance on removing local connection policies (not a requirement) had also meant that some authorities had taken a less *"parochial attitude"* (Audit Commission, [2009], p. 18).

There had also been a move from more paternalistic approaches to services in some areas. The *"...culture of inclusiveness, partnership working and consultation..."* (Audit Commission, 2009, p. 19) within the programme is credited with this. Examples are given where service users and ex-service users have acted as peer reviewers. There is also a suggestion that use of service users in procurement has led to improvements in value for money (VFM) and outcomes.

Local and national governance arrangements enabled a structured framework to involve service users and providers. The quality assessment framework and performance monitoring system enabled consistent benchmarking across providers and service areas and empowered local administration to monitor and improve value for money and challenge poor performers to improve. In addition, the ring-fenced grant allowed reinvestment of savings into new services.

There were, however, a number of areas where improvements were required. The strategic direction of the programme had been weakened by a lack of consistency starting from central government and embedded at local level. Stability of funding became an issue due to a perception that the legacy-funding amount was too high; the associated reductions combined with the proposal to remove the ring-fence threatened the viability of services. Finally, the regulation of services was also inconsistent and SP teams and providers struggled to balance costs and benefits. These factors were combined with some perverse incentives that meant poorer performing authorities often received additional resources whilst better the better performers were making cuts.

Supporting People, as a policy, had many positive effects on the supported living sector. It provided a much needed and considerable injection of funding and resources into the sector that had historically been low on the government agenda for this. It also provided a framework for the strategic commissioning of services so that supply could be modelled to meet demand within local authority areas, and to a degree between local authorities, particularly in London where there was some excellent joint working. The programme also delivered a robust and well-appreciated framework for assessing and improving the quality of services (the QAF). Providers interviewed (Irving-Clarke, 2016) spoke particularly highly of this and its role in improving services and the sector as a whole. However, there were also many areas of weakness (highlighted above), and it is here that there is real value in that they allow us as both theorists and practitioners to make recommendations for how things may be done differently in the future.

The coalition and conservative policy (2010 to the present)

Main implementation style – hybrid top-down/bottom-up
Philosophical underpinning – return to 2nd way/neo-liberalism

Following a relatively intense period of policy for supported housing under New Labour, the coalition largely left it alone. Like their Thatcherite predecessors, their main concern was value for money. Changes to supported housing policy by the coalition and then Conservative governments have formed part of a wider scheme of welfare reform. Although it has been argued that the residualisation of the poorest and most vulnerable has been in train for some years (Malpass & Victory, 2010; Mullins & Murie, 2006), Fitzpatrick and Pawson (2014; Fitzpatrick & Watts, 2017) and Watts and Fitzpatrick (2018) argue that since 2010 social housing in the UK has become more akin to an "ambulance service" than a general welfare service. Fitzpatrick & Pawson highlight the withdrawal of security of tenure from social housing tenants whilst Gibb (2015) carried out an early evaluation of the "Bedroom Tax" arguing that it had failed to meet stated policy goals whilst contributing to the growing insecurity of social tenants; in particular those with particular vulnerabilities such as a disability or children with special needs. Research by the Chartered Institute of Housing (CIH) (2017b) found a similar pattern of results regarding the overall benefit cap policy – the benefit cap was found to be manifestly unfair in the way it was implemented, e.g. families fostering children being capped despite acting out of good intentions.

As part of this raft of welfare reforms, in an effort to limit spending, the proposal was to make supported housing subject to the Local Housing Allowance (LHA) cap and a 1% rent reduction for four years from April 2016 (CIH, 2016). Following concerns raised by the sector, the government postponed these measures pending a review of funding for supported housing. In a written statement to the House of Commons (HCWS154) the then Secretary of State for Work and Pensions confirmed that tenants of supported housing would not be affected by the extension of LHA rates to the wider social sector until 2019/2020.

The proposed measures from 2019 to 2020 were that supported housing would be subject to the LHA cap where rents were paid via HB or Universal Credit. However, rents would not be subject to the Shared Accommodation Rate (SAR), a rate that limits single people under 35 years to a sum sufficient to rent a room in a shared house. To mitigate the concerns raised by the sector, the government also proposed giving local authorities a ring-fenced fund to "top-up" local supported housing services. This fund would take account of projected need and spend on providing and commissioning of services. This funding was solely to cover rent and service charges, however, support charges remained in the ambit of general local authority grant.

There would also be a full consultation on the funding of supported housing, this would look at projections of future need, mechanisms for funding the development of new supported housing, a mechanism for ensuring that top-up funding continues to be spent on developing/providing supported housing, levels of funding required to enable local authorities to administer the new arrangements, options to reform the regulation of supported housing and measures to ensure that this is both effective and proportionate (CIH, 2016). Following this consultation, the government came back with the following proposals.

Sheltered rent

As established previously, sheltered (and Extra Care) housing is primarily for older people (generally thought of as over 65, but age restrictions have been decreasing) (CIH, 2017a; Parry & Thompson, 2005). In line with predictions for, and the reality of, an ageing population, the government (and others) anticipate that demand for this type of housing will only increase (CIH, 2017a). The government's proposal for this type of housing was to put in place a "sheltered rent".

This was to be a type of social rent paid for via the welfare system and including both eligible rent charges and service charges. To meet the requirement for spending control in the consultation (CLG, 2017a), this new type of rent was to be regulated by the social housing Regulator and a cap put in place according to a formula (never determined), annual increases in the rent amount would also have been capped. Existing sheltered housing schemes (with existing rent charges) would be brought into the system at these existing levels; with new schemes subject to the new "sheltered rent" immediately. In rent setting, the "reasonableness" of rents and service charges would continue to be assessed under Section 19 of the *Landlord and Tenant Act 1985* (CIH, 2017b). This was welcome in that it provided continuity for providers.

Sector concerns

In their response to the consultation (MHCLG, 2018), the government set down the key concerns they had heard from the supported housing sector. In terms of long-term services. There was understanding from the sector not only about concerns about value for money but also concerns about the unintended consequences of the proposed definition and the ability of providers to recover their full costs.

The government acknowledged great diversity in the sector and the diversity in rents and service charges. Many rents in this housing type were already set by formula; eligible service charges varied according to service type, furnishings, buildings, design type and other factors. The government acknowledged the complexity of setting a ceiling rent – setting the ceiling too high would have a limited impact, setting it too low would limit providers ability to fully recover costs and therefore threaten existing and future supply (MHCLG, 2018). It is also hard to escape the fact that a regime for ensuring these rents and service charges are reasonable exists via the *Landlord and Tenant Act 1985 (s.19)*, blunting government criticisms about value for money to some degree.

As a result of this, the government resolved to work with the sector on value for money but is not proceeding with their proposal for a "sheltered rent" in the forthcoming rent standard direction (*ibid*).

Short term/transitional housing

This was the area with perhaps the most radical proposals for change. Hitherto, costs in this type of housing had been met by HB (eligible rent and services charges) and Supporting People (support charges); Supporting People still exists (if only notionally) as part of the general grant to Local Authorities.

Following the consultation (which sought to define categories as well as propose solutions), this category was said to cover young people, homeless people with support needs, people feeling domestic violence and others with short term support needs, i.e. support needs that are resolvable in a short amount of time (as opposed to chronic conditions). Short term is defined as a service provided for less than two years (CIH, 2017b; DETR, 2001).

The government's proposal for these services was to put in place a local ring-fenced grant commissioned at a local level and with a new local planning and oversight regime (CIH, 2017b). In areas where there are two tiers of local government (mainly county authorities with districts and boroughs), the funding was to go to the upper-tier authority with an expectation that they work closely with the districts, boroughs and other partners. Importantly, it would now be the accommodation that is funded rather than individual resident. This has two important implications. First, it takes funding these schemes out of the ambit of HB, breaking the link between short-term services and demand-led funding administered by local authorities. This takes a demand-led (and theoretically un-ring-fenced) sum and moves it to being a cash-limited grant provided by central government to local authorities. This is clearly attractive to a central government wishing to limit costs and make the sum required predictable in future years. Second (and relatedly), it breaks the link between the individual's right to a service and the ability to claim funding to have that service provided. This is one of the main concerns of the sector about the proposals (see Crisis, 2017).

Sector concerns

In their response to the consultation responses (MHCLG, 2018), the government acknowledged the main concerns of the sector. Again, these were that there is enormous diversity in the sector making coming to both a single definition and a single funding model problematic. Providers were also concerned about the move from a demand-led model to a commissioning model for the reasons discussed.

Local authorities were said to be broadly supportive of the proposals but were concerned about the increased administrative costs of not only commissioning services but regulating them also. Providers were concerned that long-lived services would be at the risk of not receiving adequate funding, this would raise their borrowing costs and also depress supply. The sector also asked for guarantees that the grant fund would rise in future years in line with social rents and respond to increased demand.

In response, the government backed down on the proposal, committing to funding short-term services via the existing welfare system, with the proviso that a robust system of oversight would be introduced, and a review of service charges carried out to assess the complexity of this aspect of the system.

Long-term services

In contrast with short-term services, this is the area where the government made the least contentious proposals. These are services for people requiring long-term support, e.g. some older people with chronic conditions, people with learning disabilities and/or mental health problems or people with physical disabilities requiring highly specialised support. Their proposal was simply to allow funding to continue as it had; with eligible rent and service charges continuing to be met via the welfare system. The government committed to working with the sector to ensure greater cost control and quality assurance (CIH, 2017b). In all cases, the government has stated that it will work with the sector to deliver robust value for money and quality assessment tools.

References

Atkinson, D (1988) Residential care for children & adults with mental handicap in I Sinclair (ed), *Residential Care: The Research Reviewed*, London, HMSO pp. 125–156.

Audit Commission (1998) *Home Alone*, Audit Commission, London.

Audit Commission (2005) *Supporting People*, Audit Commission, London.

Audit Commission (2009) *Supporting People*, Audit Commission, London.

Baggott, R (2004) *Health and Health Care in Britain* (3rd Edition), Palgrave MacMillan, Basingstoke.

Barton, R (1959) *Institutional Neurosis*, Wright, Bristol.

Baxter, S & Carr, H (2007) *Supported Housing and the Law*, SITRA, London.

Bowl, R (1986) Social work with old people in C Phillipson & A Walker (eds), *Ageing & Social Policy*, Gower, Aldershot pp. 128–145.

Busch-Geertsema, V & Sahlin, I (2007) The role of hostels and temporary accommodation, *European Journal of Homelessness* 1 pp. 67–93.

Cameron, A (2009) Working across boundaries to improve health outcomes: A case study of a housing support and outreach service for homeless people living with HIV, *Health and Social Care in the Community* 17 pp. 388–395.

CIH (2016) *What You Need to Know About the Future Funding of Supported Housing*, CIH, Coventry.

CIH (2017a) *Feeling the Pinch: The Benefit Cap One Year On*, CIH, Coventry.

CIH (2017b) *What You Need to Know About Government Proposals to Fund Supported Housing*, CIH, Coventry.

CLG (2007) *Independence and Opportunity – Our Strategy for Supporting People*, CLG, London.

CLG (2008a) *Changing Supporting People Funding in England: Results from a Pilot Exercise*, CLG, London.

CLG (2008b) *Needs Analysis, Commissioning and Procurement for Housing Related Support*, CLG, London.

CLG (2008c) *Housing, Care, Support: A Guide to Integrating Housing-related Support at Regional Level*, CLG, London.

CLG (2008d) *Research into the Effectiveness of Floating Support Services for the Supporting People Programme: Final Report*, DCLG, London.

CLG (2009a) *Research into the Financial Benefits of the Supporting People Programme*, CLG, London.

CLG Committee (2009b) *The Supporting People Programme*, HMSO, London.

Cmd 6494 (1942) *The Beveridge Report*, HMSO, London.

Craigforth (2008) *Evaluation of Supporting People (Housing Support Outcomes Framework)*, Scottish Government, Edinburgh.

Crisis (2017) *Crisis Consultation Response on the Future of Supported Housing Funding*, Crisis, London.

Crowther, M (1991) *The Workhouse System, 1834–1929: The History of an English Social Institution*, Methuen, London.

CSCI (2006) *Supporting People: Lessons from Inspections*, CSCI, London.

Dean, H (2008) *Social Policy*, Polity Press, Cambridge.

DETR (2001) *Supporting People: Policy into Practice*, HMSO, London.

DHSS (1988) *The Griffiths Report*, HMSO, London.

DoH (1989) *Caring for People: Community Care in the Next Decade and Beyond*, HMSO, London.

DoH (2001) *Valuing People*, HMSO, London.

Drake, RF (2001) *The Principles of Social Policy*, Palgrave, Basingstoke.

DSS (1998) *Supporting People: A New Policy & Funding Framework for Support Services*, HMSO, London.

Eliot, J & Hamilton, N (2009) Supporting people and the future of housing related support, *Housing, Care and Support* 12 pp. 30–35.

Eyden, J (1965) The physically handicapped in D Marsh (ed), *An Introduction to the Study of Social Administration*, Routledge and Kegan Paul, London pp. 161–174.

Fitzpatrick, S & Pawson, H (2014) Ending security of tenure for social renters: Transitioning to 'Ambulance Service' social housing?, *Housing Studies* 29(5) pp. 597–615.

Fitzpatrick, S & Watts, B (2017) Competing visions: Security of tenure and the welfarisation of English social housing, *Housing Studies* 32(8) pp. 1021–1038.

Foord, M & Simic, P (2005) *Housing, Community Care and Supported Housing – Resolving Contradictions*, CIH, Coventry.

Foucault, M (1977) *Discipline and Punish: The Birth of the Prison*, Random House, New York.

Foucault, M (Rainbow, P [ed]) (1997) *Ethics, Subjectivity and Truth*, New Press, New York.

Fyson, R et al. (2007) *Support for Living: The Impact of the Supporting People Programme on Housing and Support for Adults with Learning Disabilities*, Joseph Rowntree Foundation, New York.

Gibb, K (2015) The multiple policy failures of the bedroom tax, *International Journal of Housing Policy* 15(2) pp. 148–166.

Gibbons, J (1998) Residential care for Mentally Ill adults in I Sinclair (ed), *Residential Care: The Research Reviewed*, HMSO, London pp. 157–197.

Goffman, E (1961) *Asylums: Essays on the Social Situation of Mental Patients and Other Inmates*, Penguin, London.

Goffman, E (1970) *Stigma: Notes on the Management of Spoiled Identity*, Penguin, London.

Goldie, N (2004) *The Supporting People Programme and Mental Health*, Sainsbury Centre for Mental Health, London.

Goodwin, S (1990) *Community Care and the Future of Mental Health Service Provision*, Avebury, Aldershot.

Hadley, R & Clough, R (1996) *Care in Chaos: Frustration & Challenge in Community Care*, Cassell, London.

Hall, PA (1993) Policy paradigms, social learning and the state: The case of economic policy making in Britain, *Comparative Politics* 25(3) pp. 275–296.

Harrison, F (1986) *The Young Disabled Adult: The Use of Residential Homes and Hospital Units for People Aged 16–64*, Royal College of Physicians, London.

Hawley, K & Hudson, B (1996) *Community Care and the Prospects for Service Development*, King's Fund, London.

HCWS154 (2016) *Housing Benefit Written Statement to the House of Commons* by the Secretary of State for Work and Pensions made on September 15, 2016.

Holman, P (2008) *Putting the support in supporting people, Learning Disabilities Today* 20 (2).

Irving-Clarke (2016) *Supporting people – How did we get here and what does it mean for the future?* Unpublished PhD thesis, De Montfort University, Leicester.

Jones, K (1972) *A History of the Mental Health Services*, Routledge & Kegan & Paul, London.

Jones, A & Pleace, N (2010) *A Review of Single Homelessness in the UK*, Crisis and Joseph Rowntree Foundation, London.

Kay, A (2005) A critique of the use of path dependency in policy studies, *Public Administration* 83(3) pp. 553–571.

Leat, D (1998) Residential care for younger physically disabled adults in I Sinclair (ed), *Residential Care: The Research Reviewed*, HMSO, London pp. 199–239.

Lewis, J & Glennerster, H (1996) *Implementing the New Community Care*, Open University Press, Buckingham.

MacNicol, J (2006) *Age, Discrimination: An Historical and Contemporary Analysis*, Cambridge University Press, Cambridge.

Malin, N et al. (1980) *Services for the Mentally Handicapped in Britain*, Croom Helm, London.

Malpass, P & Murie, A (1999) *Housing Policy & Practice*, MacMillan, Basingstoke.

Malpass, P & Victory, C (2010) The modernisation of social housing in England, *International Journal of Housing Policy* 10(1) pp. 3–18.

Martin, M (1995) Medical knowledge and medical practice: Geriatric knowledge in the 1950s, *Social History of Medicine* 7(3) pp. 443–461.

Means, R et al. (2008) *Community Care* (4th Edition), Palgrave MacMillan, Basingstoke.

MHCLG (2018) *Funding for Supported Housing: Government Response to Two Consultations*, HMSO, London.

Miller, E & Gwynne, G (1972) *A Life Apart*, Tavistock, London.

Morris, P (1969) *Put Away: A Sociological Study of Institutions for the Mentally Retarded*, Routledge & Kegan & Paul, London.

Mullins, D & Murie, A (2006) *Housing Policy in the UK*, MacMillan, Basingstoke.

Murphy, E (1991) *After the Asylums: Community Care for People with Mental Illness*, Faber & Faber, London.

Neale, J (1997) Homelessness and Theory Reconsidered, *Housing Studies* 12(1) pp. 47–71.

Newman, J (2001) *New Labour, Policy and Society*, SAGE, London.

Newman, J (2014) Landscapes of antagonism: Local governance, neoliberalism and austerity, *Urban Studies* 51(15) pp. 3290–3305.

Nuffield Provincial Hospitals Trust (1946) *The Hospital Surveys: The Domesday Book of the Hospital Services*, Oxford University Press, Oxford.

Pannell & Thomas (1999) *Almshouses into the Next Millenium: Paternalism, Partnership, Progress*, Policy Press, Bristol.

Parker, J (1965) *Local Health and Welfare Services*, Allen and Unwin, London.

Parry, I & Thompson, L (2005) *Sheltered and Retirement Housing: A Good Practice Guide*, CIH, Coventry.

Parton, N (1991) *Governing the Family*, MacMillan, Basingstoke.

Pearce, D (2007) Family, gender & class in psychiatric patient care during the 1930s: The 1930 mental treatment act and the Devon mental hospital in P Dale & J Melling (eds), *Mental Illness and Learning Disability since 1850: Finding a Place for Mental Disorder in the UK*, Routledge, London pp. 112–130.

Rhodes, RAW (1997) *Understanding Governance: Policy Networks, Governance, Reflexivity and Accountability*, OU Press, Buckingham.

Robb, B (1967) *Sans Everything: A Case to Answer*, University of Michigan, Nelson.

Robson Rhodes (2004) *Independent Review of the Supporting People Programme*, DCLG, London.

Rowntree Report (1980) *Old People: Report of a Survey Committee on the Problems of Ageing and the Care of Old People*, Arnbo Press, New York.

Rummery, K (2002) *Disability, Citizenship & Community Care: A Case for Welfare Rights*, Ashgate, Aldershot.

Rummery, K & Glendinning, C (1999) Negotiating needs, access and gatekeeping: Developments of health and community care policy in the UK and the rights of disabled & older citizens, *Critical Social Policy* 19(3) pp. 335–351.

Ryan, J & Thomas, E (1980) *The Politics of Mental Handicap*, Penguin, Hammondsworth.

Samson, E (1994) *Old Age in the New World*, Pilot Press, London.

Secretary of State (2010) *Government Response to the House of Commons and Local Government Select Committee Report into the Supporting People Programme*, HMSO, London.

Scragg, T (2008) Reflections on supporting people: A Case Study of Outreach-3Way, *Housing, Care and Support* 11 pp. 16–19.

Scull, A (1993) *The Most Solitary of Afflictions: Madness and Society in Britain 1700–1900*, Yale University Press, New Haven, CT.

Seddon, J (2008) *Systems Thinking in the Public Sector*, Triarchy Press, Axminster.

SITRA (2014) *Navigating the Maze – Housing Related Support: A Guide on Engaging with and Influencing Local Governance and Commissioning Structures*, SITRA, London.

Sumner, G & Smith, R (1969) *Planning Local Authority Services for the Elderly*, George, Allen & Unwin, London.

Topliss, E (1979) *Provision for the Disabled* (2nd Edition), Blackwell, Oxford.

Townsend, P (1964) *The Last Refuge*, Routledge and Kegan Paul, London.

Tredgold, A (1952) *A Textbook on Mental Deficiency*, Balliere, Tindall and Cox, London.

Watson, L et al. (2003) *Supporting People: Real Change?* Joseph Rowntree Foundation, New York.

Watts, B & Fitzpatrick, S (2018) *Welfare Conditionality*, Routledge, Abingdon.

5 Supported housing –
the future

The future policy direction of Supported Housing is unclear at the present time. The Government has stated it is committed to the provision and funding of supported housing and has rolled back on its recent proposals for funding changes following concerns raised by the sector (CIH, 2017; MHCLG, 2018). The sector awaits government proposals regarding value for money and regulation frameworks. This being the case, now is an excellent time to consider the lessons of the past and what these tell us about the potential way forward.

The basic policy paradigm of providing supported housing has not changed much in that there has been an ongoing acceptance that assistance from state to vulnerable people or those in poverty is both desirable and necessary. The key movements have been from the pre-World War 2 position of self-help and the deterrence from poverty of the workhouse and asylums, to the post-war settlement and Beveridge's vision of the welfare state, to the Thatcher reforms of the 1990s and marketisation of the sector. The 1990s onward saw the establishment and expansion of duties upon local authorities to provide housing to certain groups deemed vulnerable and subsequent expansion of hostel accommodation to provide the temporary accommodation required in the *Housing Act 1996* and *Homelessness Act 2002*. There were also developments in the definition of "vulnerability" in other arenas, but these definitions largely related to eligibility for statutory social care services rather than housing. New Labour added their own contribution via the third-way vision of the sector implemented via the Supporting People programme. The coalition and Conservative governments since 2010 have returned to Thatcherite themes of value for money and market-driven policies.

This history contains some "moments" where change was possible and even thought desirable; such as the Industrial Revolution or outbreak and consequences of two world wars. There have been periods where politicians have favoured some groups over others depending on the political priorities of the time. There have been "moments" where huge capital investment, e.g. building asylums or huge ethos changes, e.g. NHS and *Community Care Act 1990* have made reversal or changing path difficult or impossible as suggested by Pierson (2000). Most significantly in terms of path dependency, the pattern has largely been one of Marsh and Rhodes' (1992) "diminishing returns" with numerous policy initiatives not being delivered by those charged with implementation. There has been a consistent failure to provide adequate support for vulnerable people. There are several contributing factors to this failure.

As industrialisation advanced and rural production decreased, those with disabilities found themselves less and less able to contribute to the economy/play a role in production. This led to people with disabilities, physical or mental; to be seen as a problem and therefore they were either institutionalised away from productive society or pensioned off to keep them out of the workforce (Means et al., 1998). These minority groups have also been deprived of a political voice (Murphy, 1991). Because of this, the welfare of these groups has often been viewed as a fringe policy area and this has been reflected in the appointment of junior ministers to advocate policy and lack of commitment to improving services, if not in the resources committed. The results of two world wars have also relegated these groups to the margins of policy as priority was given to the injured and psychologically damaged victims of war. Vulnerable groups had little political influence and so found themselves unable to raise awareness of their plight or do much about it. The perception of these groups remains a negative one, although this is improving.

Services for vulnerable people have often straddled several government departments and been victim to large-scale reorganisations; they have been required to change constantly to fit in. Because of this, at all levels there has been a failure to build adequate "policies" and "institutions" (see Kay, 2005) as protection from contingent events or reorganisations. Indeed, these services have been the victim of other processes that have locked in alternative paths.

Murphy's (1991) point about powerful psychiatric consultants is a case in point. She identifies the focus of psychiatrists on those with short-term illnesses that were curable with interest in those with long-term conditions beginning to fade. Treatment centred on wards in psychiatric and teaching hospitals and psychiatrists often had offices in these hospitals and some distance from the long-term institutions. This led to a two-tier system of treatment. Murphy (1991) believes that many psychiatrists adopted a medical model of mental health of which rehabilitation wasn't a part and didn't think that merely maintaining those with long-term conditions was the role of a doctor. These consultant psychiatrists also held considerable power and were loathe giving up their fiefdoms to other professions who may have been better placed to rehabilitate patients, e.g. psychologists, occupational therapists and nurses (*ibid*). Services for those with mental health issues and learning disabilities are characterised by long periods of inaction and neglect of service users interspersed by times of optimism and concerted action by policymakers to improve conditions. However, those delivering services have not followed this through on the ground.

In tandem with local authority restructures, central government has sought to limit the power of local authorities by limiting the power they have to raise and spend money locally. Murphy (1991) is clear that good, local community care services are dependent upon willing and able local authorities with the power to spend money on providing suitable housing and services. To go back to an earlier point, as large hospitals closed and discharged patients, local authorities were either unwilling or unable to start up community-based services to take up treatment. The agenda from central government to limit local government expenditure coupled with the agenda to shift responsibility for providing community care services onto local authorities created a perverse financial disincentive to expanding community-based services. To put it simply, responsibility for providing services shifted, but the ability to raise and/or spend money to do so was removed.

At a high level, there have been real issues with the lack of a coherent definition of and legal duties to vulnerable people who did not meet the threshold for social care but required support to live independently and a resulting lack of services. For people who fell under the local authority duty to provide housing, there was not a corresponding duty to provide the support that they needed to maintain their accommodation and live independently. This led to tenancy failure and repeat homelessness. This is also a problem for ensuring people who fall between eligibility for social care and priority need for housing but still require support to maintain a tenancy or accommodation. This includes people and families who would be owed a housing duty but are found intentionally homeless or to have no local connection.

There has also been a long-term failure to provide adequate community-based services (Murphy, 1991). Attempting to explain this failure and as an argument against developing them, some academics and clinicians have argued that to do so would undermine the support from family and friends and that this in turn would fuel a massive expansion in state services. The opposing view is of course that not offering support may cause some families to prematurely give up this caring and supporting role and thus fuel the need for greater levels of support and care. Means et al. (2008, p. 47) illustrate this argument with the use of two quotes, *"All governments assume that if you care about someone, you should be willing to care for them"* (Dalley, 1996) and *"disabled people have a right not to be made dependent upon family members and other close relatives in order to have their needs met"* (Morris, 2002).

The stereotype of older and disabled people in the UK is overall a negative one. Old age is often perceived as little more than a slide into decrepitude, disability as a debilitating condition meaning people are unable to contribute to society (Means et al., 2008). As large hospitals were emptied of the mentally ill, it was assumed that they would gradually close. However, the increasing number of older people who were either disabled or suffering from dementia then took many bed-spaces. Resources were increased but due to this expansion of care for the elderly and increase in the level of need, additional funds were taken up maintaining the level of service rather than improving it for those who remained or moved into the community (Means et al., 2008).

Despite being very different client groups, the development of services for people with physical disabilities shares many narrative aspects with that of mentally ill and elderly people. A lack of strategic planning, powers granted but not utilised and contingency/emergency situations taking priority elsewhere, led to policy outcomes that were far from what policymakers surely intended. There is a distinct pattern of institutional services provided in large, impersonal settings with low-priority status. Numerous changes to administrative structures and new powers granted to authorities providing services proved of little worth in improving the situation. Both world wars and other contingencies/crises have had a considerable effect on services both highlighting the need for better services whilst at the same time swamping services with the infirm and injured or drawing attention to other service areas.

Housing, as a policy area, entered the debate relatively recently. Poor-quality housing had pervaded society for many years. It was only in the post-war periods that there had been any serious policy to provide good-quality housing. The *National Assistance Act 1948* and *Housing (Homeless Persons) Act 1977* had ensured basic provison was available for homeless people, the latter placing a duty to provide accommodation to those deemed in "priority need". These acts, although welcome, saw the problem very much as a function of being without a roof and therefore proposed solutions on this basis – if you had a roof over your head, you were outside the scope of the act. These acts also imposed a number of tests upon homeless people under which assistance could be withdrawn, e.g. intentional homelessness or having no local connection.

Supporting People offered hope that this repeated pattern would finally be ended. A realtively huge injection of funding, in the form of a ring-fenced and initially unlimited sum, meant that local authorities and voluntary sector providers could set up new services and expand upon existing ones. Irving-Clarke (2016) found evidence that some providers went from barely being able to fund their management teams to having well-staffed human resources and IT teams, necessary to back operational demands. The creation of a quality assurance tool the Quality Assessment Framework (QAF) led to the improvement of services and was appreciated by those working in the sector who welcomed the opportunity to demonstrate the quality of their work (Irving-Clarke, 2016). The QAF also provided an independent framework by which the quality of services could be assessed, raising quality; the focus on service user involvement on the higher levels of the framework led to more and better involvement in services by those receiving them.

The programme also provided a framework to ensure that services were planned and delivered strategically. This required local authorities to assess demand for services in their areas and produce a five-year "Supporting People Strategy", they were then required to inspect all SP-funded services in their area and begin to shape provision to fit the strategy. This could be done by remodelling existing services, starting new services or shutting down services that were either of poor quality or not strategically relevant, although shutting down of services or removing funding was always said to be a less desirable action (DETR, 2001).

The Supporting People programme provided significant progress for people who required supported housing services. Audit Commission (2005, 2009) and Irving-Clarke (2016) found that there were many areas of improvement including higher quality services, better service user involvement and better strategic planning in the best performing authorities. There were however, some authorities where the programme did not become embedded (Audit Commission 2005, 2009) and even in well-performing authorities there was sometimes a lack of consistency in the way that the programme was implemented (especially the QAF) (Irving-Clarke, 2016).

Although the programme does still exist within local authorities in England (if only nominally), the beginning of the end of the programme was heralded very early in its life. Robson Rhodes (2004) investigated how the Supporting People programme had become so expensive, a final "Platinum Cut" of around £1.8 billion against an original estimate of circa £800,000. They found that some local authorities had used the programme to set up large new teams, often providing floating support; others chose not to start many new services, thus not maximising their income from the new funding. There was also evidence that some local authorities had used Supporting People (SP) funding to fund services that were not eligible, no checks were made during the initial implementation nor were they required to pay any of this money back. Robson Rhodes stated that SP funding was not being spent in the most efficient way and that more could be achieved for the money being put into the programme. They did not say that the overall sum was inappropriate to the programme's aims nor that it should be reduced, but this was how it was interpreted by the government.

A phase of cuts to funding began. The overall sum going into the programme was reduced year on year and this was reflected in cuts to local authority SP teams' funding. Local authorities responded by driving efficiencies in their areas and this often led to across the board cuts in funding rather than the strategically led funding of relevant services (Audit Commisson, 2009, Irving-Clarke, 2016). This was coupled with a failure to redistribute funding between those authorities that had maximised funding during the initial phase of the programme and those who had not. A redistribution formula had been proposed but never implemented. These funding reductions coincided with the financial crisis of 2008 meaning that the imperative to save money in government became more powerful than it had been for many years – driving further and deeper cuts to funding.

The real death knell of the programme came in 2010 with the move to "Local Area Agreements", these provided a new framework for local authority funding. Local authorities were required to produce a "Local Area Plan" for the provision and funding of local services. The importance of this is that the ring-fence on Supporting People funding was removed and it was placed within the sum granted under the Local Area Agreement funding settlements. The inevitable happened (looking back at the history of services) and local under pressure local authorities prioritised services they had a statutory duty to provide and the Supporting People programme (in England) suffered death by a thousand cuts. It still exists to a degree in Wales, Scotland and Northern Ireland, but there are regular outcries about proposed reductions to funding and future of the programme.

As we have seen in the history of services in Chapter 4, supported housing has long been a neglected area of service provision despite its very real potential for providing preventative and money-saving services. It is hard to escape the conclusion however that due to the non-statutory nature of the programme, lack of commitment to funding and provision of services that once again vulnerable people face a situation where they are of low priority for services. The Supporting People programme it seems was just another "moment" in the path of supported housing service provision where there was a real possibility for change, such change looked likely to happen, but a lack of commitment coupled with exogenous shocks in the policy environment (e.g. the financial crisis) meant that this was not followed through on.

The coalition (2010–2015) and Conservative (2015–present) have appeared ambivalent about supported housing and its potential. There have been proposals to change the way that it is funded as part of a wider "welfare reform" agendum, but the government has rolled back on these after the sector successfully raised a number of concerns about how these would threaten the future of many organisations and have deleterious effects on many service user groups. On a more positive note, the government is once again interested in social housing more widely and has committed to both social and supported housing going forward (MHCLG, 2017, 2018). This is in no small part due to the fire at the Grenfell Tower in London – this may prove to be a watershed (although unnecessary, avoidable and horrific) moment in the "path".

Supported housing and policy success

As I have gone to some lengths to show, the history of supported housing provision from the pre-Victorian age to the present has not been one of great success.

In programme terms, there have been sustained and multiple failures to provide adequate services for the vulnerable and where services are provided, they have rarely been given adequate funding or priority. In Chapter 4, there is plenty of evidence of those charged with implementing policy failing to meet the goals set down by policymakers. Vulnerable and needy people have suffered for this. In both the social care and housing policy domains there has been a long-term failure of both government policy and implementation. The policy goals in this domain have not been met. The Supporting People programme offered some hope with a ring-fenced funding stream and regulatory and strategic frameworks that were welcomed by the sector (Irving-Clarke, 2016). The removal of the ring-fence on funding all but ended the programme, another failure to build the requisite policies and institutions put forward by Kay (2005). The withdrawal of the Conservative proposals on funding is welcome but we await proposals for regulation and value-for-money initiatives.

In terms of politics, there has been a long-term failure in this domain also. Politicians have failed to give vulnerable groups and people adequate priority or protection. Conversely, vulnerable people and groups have not had the political "clout" to enforce their rights (where rights existed) or to effectively campaign for change. In addition, care and support policy has been low on the list of political priorities for politicians. Events such as the oil crisis in the 1970s or the deaths of children (Maria Colwell for example) have taken attention and funding away from unfashionable policy areas. Even the relatively successful and robust Supporting People programme was largely precipitated by a court judgement regarding what Housing Benefit could and couldn't pay for, rather than any great political will to provide services (Irving-Clarke, 2016). However, it was a robust response and fitted well with the wider third-way project of renewal and communitarian solutions.

The "process" of policy in this area has been relatively successful. There have been numerous Acts of Parliament and other policy documents that have proposed help for those in need of it. The mass building programmes of workhouses, asylums and post-war housing point to the fact that large-scale mobilisation of resources is both possible and has been desirable. However, the issue here is still one of lack of necessary priority. Legislation (with a few exceptions) has granted permissions to local authorities where it could have given duties to provide services. Where duties have been granted, this has proven effective, e.g. Housing Act 1996. Even the Supporting People programme provided no legal backstop for services, meaning that even where groups were well organised in demanding services, they had no legal recourse to enforce their rights (Irving-Clarke, 2016). There is no better example of how this played out than the removal of the ring-fence on funding from Supporting People and the highly deleterious effect this had on the programme.

Where we go from here – a blueprint...

As we await the government's proposals for a value-for-money and regulatory framework for supported housing, this section draws on the lessons learned to make recommendations for a potential way forward for services.

First, and to start at the beginning, any future policy in this area must be underpinned by a strong and robust set of clear policy goals, and these must be maintained throughout. It must also be clear that these are the criteria by which success or failure will be assessed. The experience of Supporting People was that these changed considerably over the implementation process. During interviews, professionals working in the sector sometimes needed prompting on these – they were no longer clear what these were (Irving-Clarke, 2016). There was a plethora of reviews, strategies and other documents (see Chapter 4) that either changed the objectives or added considerably to them during implementation. Whilst it is true that objectives can change over time as policies develop, having a clear set of objectives that are sustained throughout would be advantageous – everyone would know what they are trying to achieve and how.

Second, any future policy in this area requires a legislative underpinning that gives it force of law. This is because first, softer policy tools have failed to produce concerted action in the past, and second, as a human rights issue underpinned by various national and international obligations action is essential. This does not have to be a prescriptive piece of legislation that enforces what services will have to be provided, when and to whom but should rather be a piece of law or policy that brings central government, local government, providing agencies and others to coalesce around a definition of what it means to be well housed, and provide these agencies with a duty to ensure that all citizens have accommodation and services that meet this duty.

Each citizen must have the right to be securely housed, have private space to conduct relationships and the support (where needed) to take part in their community and civic society. This would address the criticisms of Fyson et al. (2007) that services focus upon support to maintain accommo-dation only and not on involvement in wider community activities. Reach-ing such a consensus and enforcing it via legislation would provide a clear framework for local authorities and service providers to commission and provide services but crucially maintain the flexibility and ability to meet local needs. This would also provide the beginnings of the "policies" and "institutions" (Kay, 2005) required for supported housing to compete on fair terms with health, social care and other statute-based services. This is not only about the need for ring-fenced funding, but also about the priority given to it by policymakers and implementers.

Third, any future policy in this area should learn from the literature around implementation and in particular Elmore (1980) in terms of allo-cating resources. Where Supporting People sought to direct resources at providers and to a lesser degree, local authorities (and this is where it was needed), any future expansions in funding should be allocated on the basis of an assessment of where these can be most effective rather than on the claims of provider organisations. Local authorities that will have a much better knowledge of local providers and circumstances should carry out this assessment. Because of the Supporting People programme and current focus on commissioning and quality assurance, providers have improved service levels but are not funded adequately and the sector has undergone a significant contraction. There is a case for focusing on the expansion of the sector on a need-led basis – were the additional resources forthcoming. Given that this is unlikely given the current austerity agenda, remodelling of the sector on a needs-led basis but within current resources would be the best alternative. Funding should be placed back within a ring-fence, this could be done even within existing resources. It is clear that supported living services have not built up the policies or institutions (Kay, 2005) re-quired to compete for funding on level terms with other statutory areas of service.

Fourth, the policy process is still remarkably linear, even in a time of complex governance structures. Policy stems from the identification of a problem that requires resolution and the solution is passed down from cen-tral government through local structures to be delivered on the front line.

Policymakers need to acknowledge the complexity of the sector if they are to be more successful in implementation. There has been a lack of a whole systems approach in this area that has led to supported housing being a parallel sector dealing with those who are hard to reach and unpopular groups (Powell, 2000). It must be acknowledged that supported housing, as a sector, is not as advanced as health, social care and education and needs to be accorded additional support to raising its status within these arenas. This is reflected in calls for "whole-systems" approaches to supported housing by Crisis (2017) and the Domestic Abuse Housing Alliance (DAHA) (Henderson, 2018).

Policymakers need to acknowledge that all organisations have their own "path" and culture and therefore fitting into a "one size fits all" policy will be problematic for many of them in the short to medium term as they make the necessary cultural shifts. Feedback loops to local and central government need improvement in order for providers to be able to provide meaningful feedback to government and feel that they are true stakeholders in the policy.

The policy world is now one of networks and governance rather than public administration and government. Rhodes' (1997) "differentiated polity" (p. 4) is very much the way that policy is now delivered. This means that policymakers and other elected officials must use political influence to exert pressure on a vast range of actors and cannot merely make authoritative decisions as once they did (Copus, 2015). There are lessons in this regard from Irving-Clarke (2014), in the No Second Night Out – Leicester project, the separation of funding, regulation and responsibility worked well precisely because it diffused power and responsibility throughout the policy network. This arrangement has forced a much better power balance between providers and the local authority and led to improved relationships and strategic partnerships. This is a model worth pursuing in the future.

Fifth, government should be careful in terms of bureaucracy and the information it asks of the providers. Seddon (2008) makes some strong criticisms of the system that are justified. SP-funded providers carry out a plethora of assessments and other paperwork but also had arbitrary limitations placed upon them. This led to a degree of "street level bureaucracy" (Lipsky, 1980) and some organisations keeping quiet about the good work they were doing, as it wasn't within their remit. An outcomes-based model would resolve this. Providing organisations with the resources they require and then judging effectiveness on outcomes rather the processes would be a better way of doing this. This began to happen in the later days of SP but needs development.

Finally, and most importantly, there needs to be a high-level review of the structures of national, regional and local government. This review should identify what legislative duties sit at what levels of government and whether these are at the best level to be most effective. It should also identify geographic issues with these services. Audit Commission (2005) found significant issues caused by the differing geographies of local authorities, PCTs (or CCGs as they now are), the Probation Service and others. There are also additional complexities where county councils were dealing with district and borough councils who hold the main housing duty under Part 7 of the *Housing Act 1996*. As with providers above, it should also be borne in mind that these organisations all have their own "path" and culture and are managing their own "landscapes of antagonism" (Newman 2014), and this creates complexity. This review must ask itself the two questions outlined by Elmore (1980), what is the ability of the organisation to deliver the target of the policy? And, what resources does the organisation need to have that effect? Such an approach would provide resources where they are best deployed and allow the best-placed organisations to deal with the problems the policy is designed to address. This approach would also reduce "failure demand" (Seddon, 2008) and provide the resources and flexibility needed to get it right first time.

Policy implementation is a complex field and it is difficult to get it right. After all, this is the real world. Especially in the field of supported housing, people are the driver of the need for policy. People are unpredictable, irrational at times and do not always agree with us, as practitioners, on what is the best course of action for them to take. Central and local governments need to get a grip of this area and ensure that they allocate the necessary resources and structures. It is imperative that we devise a support system that is fair, flexible, supportive and implemented in such a way as to provide those who can have the greatest impact with the resources and skills to do so.

In formulating future policy in this area, policymakers must take a more pragmatic approach to policymaking and look at what will work most effectively. New Labour governments in many ways rolled back the clock on delivery by relying on a top-down implementation method ("Deliverology" [Barber, 2007]) and this created problems; these are now well documented (Bower, 2016).

In future, policymakers and implementers need to reach coalition around a "human rights" based approach to housing and support and use the rights-based arguments to implement a revised structure. In the implementation of Supporting People, it was often said that legislation would remove the flexibility from local government and implementing agencies to provide services. However, this does not have to be the case. By using legislation to create and enforce a "rights-based" approach, policymakers can create an environment where the direction from government is clear but allow local government and agencies the flexibility and autonomy to best meet the needs of local circumstance and support people effectively.

This means placing duties to provide support rather than granting permissions; the analysis in Chapter 4 has shown that where permissions are granted, action does not necessarily follow. Duties are far more likely to produce action. This requires an underlying piece of primary legislation that sets out these duties in line with Kay's (2005) ideas about creating "policies" and "institutions". Where the Supporting People programme provided a coherent policy framework for supported housing, this has taken a backward step under the coalition and Conservative governments since. The proposed value-for-money and regulation framework may address this, but it very much remains to be seen. The new framework also needs to ensure that local authorities plan strategically and that the services needed are available and (once again) adequately funded. There needs to be attention paid to the balance of services to ensure a postcode lottery does not develop in the sector. Again, strategic planning is an area that the proposed framework may address.

Supported housing, as a policy area, must have an adequate, ring-fenced funding stream for care and support that cannot be directed to other initiatives or contingent events, cannot divert funding or priority from the programme. With this is mind it is also important that services have the priority status that they require and deserve.

References

Audit Commission (2005) *Supporting People*, Audit Commission, London.
Audit Commission (2009) *Supporting People*, Audit Commission, London.
Barber, M (2007) *Instruction to Deliver*, Methuen, London.
Bower, T (2016) *Broken Vows: Tony Blair – The Tragedy of Power*, Faber & Faber, London.
CIH (2017) *What You Need to Know About Government Proposals to Fund Supported Housing*, CIH, Coventry.
Copus, C (2015) Ideology or realism in local governance: A case of RealLokal-Politik in English local government, *Croation and Comparative Public Administration*, 15(2) pp. 335–356.
Crisis (2017) *Crisis Consultation Response on the Future of Supported Housing Funding*, Crisis, London.
Dalley, G (1996) *Ideologies of Caring: Rethinking Community & Collectivism*, MacMillan, Basingstoke.
DETR (2001) *Supporting People: Policy into Practice*, HMSO, London.
Elmore, RF (1980) Backward mapping: Implementation research and policy decisions, *Political Science Quarterly* 94(4) pp. 601–616.
Fyson et al. (2007) *Support for Living: The Impact of the Supporting People Programme on Housing and Support for Adults with Learning Disabilities*, Joseph Rowntree Foundation, New York.
Henderson, K (2018) *The role of housing in a co-ordinated, community response to domestic abuse*, Unpublished PhD thesis, University of Durham, Durham.

Irving-Clarke (2014) *Towards Ending Homelessness in Leicester*, Action Homeless, Leicester.

Irving-Clarke (2016) *Supporting people – How did we get here and what does it mean for the future?* Unpublished PhD thesis, De Montfort University, Leicester.

Kay, A (2005) A critique of the use of path dependency in policy studies, *Public Administration* 83(3) pp. 553–571.

Lipsky, M (1980) *Street Level Bureaucracy: Dilemmas of the Individual in Public Services*, Russell Sage Foundation, New York.

Marsh, D & Rhodes, RAW (1992) *Policy Networks in British Government*, Clarendon Press, Wooton-Under-Edge.

Means et al. (2008) *Community Care* (4th Edition), Palgrave MacMillan, Basingstoke.

MHCLG (2017) *Funding Supported Housing: Policy Statement and Consultation*, HMSO, London.

MHCLG (2018) *Funding for Supported Housing: Government Response to Two Consultations*, HMSO, London.

Morris, J (2002) *Young Disabled People: Moving into Adulthood*, Joseph Rowntree Foundation, New York.

Murphy, E (1991) *After the Asylums: Community Care for People with Mental Illness*, Faber & Faber, London.

Newman, J (2014) Landscapes of Antagonism: Local governance, neoliberalism and austerity, *Urban Studies* 51(15) pp. 3290–3305.

Pierson, P (2000) Increasing returns: Path dependence and the study of politics, *The American Political Studies Review* 94(2) pp. 251–267.

Powell, M (2000) New labour and the third way in the British welfare state: A new and distinct approach? *Critical Social Policy* 94(2) pp. 39–60.

Rhodes, RAW (1997) *Understanding Governance: Policy Networks, Governance, Reflexivity and Accountability*, OU Press, Buckingham.

Robson Rhodes (2004) *Independent Review of the Supporting People Programme*, CLG, London.

Seddon, J (2008) *Systems Thinking in the Public Sector*, Triarchy Press, Axminster.

Index

For Product Safety Concerns and Information please contact our EU
representative GPSR@taylorandfrancis.com Taylor & Francis Verlag GmbH,
Kaufingerstraße 24, 80331 München, Germany

Batch number: 08153772

Printed by Printforce, the Netherlands